Attitude

Attitude

by Barbara Babbit Kaufman

Longstreet Press

Nancy —
"Attitude" is it —
Make it a habit —
one day at time —

Barbara Kaufman

Published by
Longstreet Press
2974 Hardman Court
Atlanta, Georgia 30305

Printed in The United States of America
1st Printing, 2004

ISBN: 1-56532-731-6

Book and jacket design by Burtch Hunter Design, LLC

For my parents, my husband and my children who motivate me everyday to be the best I can be.

Contents

INTRODUCTION

The 92-year-old, petite, well-poised and proud lady, who is fully dressed each morning by eight o'clock, with her hair fashionably coifed and makeup perfectly applied, even though she is legally blind, moved to a nursing home today.

Her husband of 70 years recently passed away, making the move necessary.

After many hours of waiting patiently in the lobby of the nursing home, she smiled sweetly when told her room was ready.

As she maneuvered her walker to the elevator, I provided a visual description of her tiny room, including the eyelet sheets that had been hung on her window.

"I love it," she stated with the enthusiasm of an eight-year-old having just been presented with a new puppy.

"Mrs. Jones, you haven't seen the room... just wait."

"That doesn't have anything to do with it," she replied. "Happiness is something you decide on ahead of time. Whether I like my room or not doesn't depend on how the furniture is arranged... it's how I arrange my mind. I already decided to love it."

"It's a decision I make every morning when I wake up."

I have a choice; I can spend the day in bed recounting the difficulty I have with the parts of my body that no longer work, or get out of bed and be thankful for the ones that do.

What is Attitude?

Life can be a bowl of cherries or the pits.
It's your choice, you get to choose.

~ ERMA BOMBECK

THE FIRST TIME I WAS ASKED TO MAKE A SPEECH, I was literally scared out of my mind. I was the founder and CEO of a high-profile retail chain of bookstores, a woman in control of my own business. I knew that speaking about my business would be great publicity for the company. I knew I wanted to do this, but in order to do so I would have to overcome my longtime fear of public speaking. Becoming a regular public speaker was a major personal goal, but actually getting in front of people and making a speech would be far from easy for me.

If I said yes to making the speech, I knew I would have to "make it happen," as I like to say. I would have to prepare a winning speech, and practice my delivery again and again until it was perfect. If I said no, I knew I would not be moving forward. I would not be working toward a goal I had always wanted to accomplish. I would be giving in to my doubts and fears.

I really wanted to make the speech. But how?

I turned to the same tool that I had used many times before to squelch other fears in my life, like going off to college, getting married, having children and starting my own business: ATTITUDE. By focusing on having **You already possess the power** a positive attitude, I was able to overcome my fear of public speaking. I knew that I could do anything I set my mind to. I could do it, because I had the right attitude—despite my fears.

And that is what this book is all about—developing and using a positive attitude to do what you want, get what you want and go where you want. Wherever that may be!

Discover the Secret to Making Change Happen

Do you often find yourself wishing you could make your life just a little bit better? Maybe you just want to change one thing, but you can't ever seem to make it happen. Or maybe you want to change many things, to be happier in your job, be happier in your life, make a bit more money, go on a great date, meet new people, find the next great idea, lose a few pounds. We all have these desires at some point in our lives.

In this book, you will discover the secret to make it happen, and the secret is that you already possess the power to do just about anything you really want. Remember in "The Wizard of Oz," how Dorothy spent the whole movie trying to get the wizard to send her back home to Kansas? Finally, after all that wandering and dangerous adventure, she discovered she didn't need a wizard to get back home, that she had the power all along to get where she wanted to go—the ruby slippers on her own feet. In *Attitude,* I'm going to show you that **you're already wearing your own pair of ruby slippers—your attitude.**

Attitude is how you approach life

What Is Attitude?

The dictionary's definition of attitude is "a state of mind or a feeling." But I believe it is so much more than that. Attitude is how you think about yourself, your life, what you do every day, how you carry yourself physically and emotionally, and how you react. Attitude is how you approach life, and your attitude will have the greatest impact on how your life plays out.

I know from my own experience that a positive attitude can make your life better. I am not more blessed than anyone else, or more beautiful or more brilliant, but I discovered that an upbeat attitude would take me places I wanted to go. I didn't need the world's greatest brain, or the luckiest break. I just needed to face each situation with an attitude that turned things to my advantage.

Scientific studies are now proving the power of attitude. A recent study conducted at the University of Wisconsin showed that the part of the human brain associated with negative emotions played a role in weakening people's response to a flu vaccine. So if a negative attitude might increase your odds of getting the flu, imagine what a positive attitude might help you overcome!

The right attitude can make almost anything possible, and the wrong attitude can make things nearly impossible. Gordon Smith, a 26-year veteran of the U.S. Army's Special Forces, once said to a reporter: "If you have a guy with all the survival training in the world who has a negative attitude, and a guy who doesn't have a clue but has a positive attitude, I guarantee you that the one with the positive attitude is coming out of the woods alive. Simple as that." Having a great attitude can help you overcome any shortcomings or any difficult situation.

The one with the positive attitude is coming out of the woods alive

You *Can* Learn a Great Attitude

I didn't start out with this fantastic attitude—I learned it! I worked on it and made it a habit, just like brushing my teeth every day or going to the gym. Just like anyone else, I've lived through challenges and obstacles, but I learned how to overcome them with a positive attitude.

When I was a teenager, I was terribly insecure. I had a weight problem. I wasn't the richest, prettiest or smartest girl in school. Lacking confidence in myself, I often had a fearful, negative attitude about life. This attitude affected me greatly as I grew older, and often caused me to face life with anxiety. Eventually, I learned to overcome my insecurities and to take action to change my negative approaches to positive ones. When I faced adversity, I learned to react with hope and optimism, and I dedicated myself to changing what could be changed.

I survived a difficult, painful divorce after many years of marriage and having two children—and I found love and happiness with a new husband. I've been fired from jobs three times in my life, and these experiences taught me important lessons about dealing with adversity and how to find what I really wanted to do.

I learned to put my attitude to work for me. Let me tell you more about where I began. After college, I became a CPA and started working in public accounting in the tax department. This base in business prepared me for my ultimate goal: to be an entrepreneur and a retailer. In the 1970s, there weren't many women in public accounting, and there weren't very many female entrepreneurs. A few months after the birth of my first daughter (I later had another daughter), I moved closer to my goal by becoming the Chief Financial Officer of Turtle's Music, a major record store chain that I co-founded. I left Turtle's when it was sold to start my other businesses, including a women's clothing store, and a children's clothing store, and ultimately, I founded and became President and CEO of Chapter 11 The Discount Bookstore, a successful chain of bookstores.

Recently, I sold Chapter 11 to pursue new business and life opportunities, and I have found many new challenges. I regularly speak to audiences about being a successful woman in business, I host a local television show in Atlanta, I consult for major companies and work as a business "executive-in-residence" at Georgia State University. In addition, I find time to be active in the community (I serve on the boards of directors of several organizations) and sports (I compete in duathlons, half marathons and other athletic events). I enjoy a full marriage, and am still actively involved with my children's lives as they move forward in their own careers.

I believe strongly that my attitude has been the key factor in making all these dreams happen, and I believe that a great attitude will help you make your dreams come true too.

I see people every day who are smart and talented, but they struggle to do some of the same things I have

My secret? I'm giving it to you now: ATTITUDE

done. They often ask me for my secret. I'm giving it you now: ATTITUDE. It's not your weight, looks, brains or luck. Fine-tune your attitude and the picture of success becomes clear.

I believe, based on my experience in business and in life, that you can change almost anything in your life for the better by using the power you have within. Perhaps you can't make drastic changes to your job, your bank account, your waistline or your love life in an instant, but you *can* change your life, improving many aspects of it so you become happier, more fulfilled, more empowered and more in control of what happens to you. You can feed positive energy into your life and approach life in a more positive way—even when facing challenges.

Yes, many things are beyond your control. Bad things do happen, even to good people who don't deserve them. Your company might eliminate your job or go into bankruptcy. Your boss might be a jerk. Your mother might get sick and need long-term care. Your marriage might fall apart. Your next-door neighbor might install a new sprinkler system that malfunctions and floods your basement. You can't change those things or keep them from happening, but you can change one important thing—how you react. You can change your *attitude.*

You can change almost anything in your life for the better by using the power you have within

Attitude is the one thing you do control, and it's the most powerful gift you have at your disposal. Attitude is everything. It's all you really need to know. Success begins and ends with attitude.

Almost everyone experiences tough times. Some people survive incredible challenges and emerge victorious, usually due to a strong positive outlook. Patricia Neal, the Academy Award™ winning actress and star of "Hud," suffered a stroke months into a pregnancy and was in a coma for 21 days. Her daughter was born healthy, but the star faced a daunting physical recovery —with a new-born. Neal later noted that a positive attitude was key to her rehabilitation and her return to acting: "A strong positive mental attitude will create more miracles than any wonder drug."

What You'll Learn in This Book

In this book, I'm going to show you some terrific techniques you can use to train yourself to have a better attitude. I use these every day and apply them to every situation I encounter. Attitude is your ultimate energy source for a better life. You can tap into it anytime you need it, to give yourself the power to go wherever you want.

Ask yourself something, and be honest: Are you always upbeat and using your energy in the most positive way? If not, you should be. I'll show you how you can be in a good mood more often. You can train yourself – with the help of the approaches in this book – to shape a more positive attitude that you can use to make the most of every day.

People often ask me why I'm in such a good mood all the time. They may think that I am upbeat because I have had some great luck in life, or that I was just **Attitude is** born confident and happy. But that isn't the **your ultimate** case. A long time ago I realized that it takes **energy** energy to be in a good mood, and it takes energy **source.** to be in a bad mood. So if it takes the same amount of energy to be in a good mood as it does to be in a bad mood, why not channel that energy into a good mood? This book will help you train yourself to have fewer bad days and to react more positively more often so you can make the most of every moment. Life is full of great opportunities that should be faced with a positive outlook and a smile.

First you must focus on your priorities and really get in touch with what changes you want to make. Once you decide where you want to go, you'll see how the approaches in this book will help get you there. As a bonus, I'll show you how your attitude can be enhanced by your physical health and fitness, and I'll share some of my own guidelines for getting into better shape and looking your best.

I'm constantly amazed at the progress people can make with just a small adjustment to their attitude. Nothing happens overnight, but you can transform your

> **"So if it takes the same amount of energy to be in a good mood as it does to be in a bad mood, why not channel that energy into a good mood?"**

vision of the future pretty quickly with a new attitude. You can do it, one little step at a time, one day at a time. A positive attitude makes facing each day just a little bit easier. With that boost, you can finally take that first step forward. Let's start right now!

At the end of each chapter, I'll include a few questions to help you identify your starting point, your challenges, your goals and how you plan to achieve them.

Take a few moments to write down your thoughts and responses to these questions.

- What is the most important thing you want in your life that you don't currently have?

- What would make you happy today? Tomorrow? Are these realistic goals—things you really have a chance to accomplish (not winning the lottery)?

- What are three to five more changes you would like to make in your life, in addition to the most important thing?

- When you face a challenge or a rejection, what is your first reaction? How do you feel one day later? A week later?

- What do you perceive to be the biggest challenges to getting what you want?

Make it Happen

A journey of 1,000 miles
begins with a single step.

~ MAHATMA GANDHI

I AM CONVINCED THAT A POSITIVE ATTITUDE CAN take you anywhere you want to go. But it's not a free ride. You have to do your part. The things you desire won't fall into your lap through magic or luck – you'll have to make them happen. Dorothy didn't get back to Kansas just by putting on the shoes – she had to click her heels, repeat "there's no place like home," and make it happen!

Begin your journey by focusing on what you really want to change or accomplish in your life. Clarify what your ultimate goal is, whether it's finding a great new job, falling in love or running a marathon. Make sure you are being realistic—don't focus on winning millions in a sweepstakes as the solution to all your problems. Once you focus on your important goal, then you're ready to take the next step and do it. That's what this chapter is all about.

You may have spent countless hours thinking about the things you would like to do, but somehow you never get started. You procrastinate. I did the same thing with this book. I thought about it when I was driving around in my car, I thought about it when I was in the shower, and I thought about it before I fell asleep at night.

Focus on what you really want
I thought about the book's content and what the end result would be, but I didn't get started. Every day I would do anything except begin to write the book. I would even do things I didn't like doing, like cleaning out my closets. I was avoiding the challenge of writing the book that I sincerely wanted to write. Why? Because I had never tried to write a book before. I was scared. I wondered, Can I do it? Will it be good? Will anyone want to read it? So instead of sit-

ting down at the keyboard and trying to start writing, I just put it off.

Finally, I decided I had to follow my own advice. If I intended to write a book on attitude and one of the first chapters was "Make It Happen," I had to make this book happen. It was not going to write itself or appear through magic. I had to begin.

The "Make It Happen" Mantra

For motivation, I used the same technique I have used to face many other challenges in my life. When I have a new idea or face a challenge, I repeat these words to myself: "Make it happen, make it happen, make it happen." I focus intensely on what I have to do, and I convince myself to overcome any obstacles and really *do it*—not just to sit around and think about doing it.

Make it happen, make it happen, make it happen

"Make it happen" is my mantra—an inspiring statement that I say over and over again to myself to give focus to my energy. By repeating "make it happen" to myself, I zero in on what I need to do to make my goal a reality. Many people use mantras to help them focus on a task and to create the internal energy to burst through their barriers and do it. My personal trainer, Matt, uses the mantra "adapt and overcome"; he repeats the phrase to himself over and over again to overcome resistance to change and to propel himself forward in challenging situations. Many people use mantras during meditation to help them shut out the negative feelings in their life and focus on the positive. Whether or not you meditate, I think it's helpful to find a mantra (you can use "make it happen" with my blessing), and pick a quiet place and time to repeat this phrase to yourself and focus on the steps you will take to achieve your goal.

I came up with my "make it happen" mantra about 20 years ago. When I was 28, I had a job working as the assistant treasurer for a mayoral campaign in Atlanta. One day I was given the task of chairing a huge event for the candidate—a gala dinner with Bill Cosby as the entertainment. This was going to be *the* major fundraising event for the campaign, and I had to make all the arrangements, including setting up the venue, arranging the food, raising money, doing the publicity and getting all the most important people to attend. I had no experience at anything like this, but suddenly I was responsible for the whole thing.

Propel yourself forward

So what did I do? I froze. I had no idea where to start. I hadn't even planned my own wedding... my mom did! But I had to do this, and I didn't want to fail.

Fortunately, just as I faced this challenging situation, a mentor—Leonard "Len" Roberts, Chairman and CEO of Radio Shack Corp.—showed me that I had the ruby slippers on my feet to get me where I needed to go. This successful businessman, who was involved in the campaign, told me, "Barbara, you have to *make it happen.* No one is going to do it for you. It's not going to fall into your lap."

He was right—I had to make it happen. I started repeating this to myself over and over again. I didn't make it happen all at once; I took baby steps to planning each portion of the big event. One phone call led to another, and led to a connection, and led to other people getting involved, and finally, the event was planned and was a huge success. We raised lots of money and our candidate won the election. More importantly for me, I learned that no matter what I had to do, I could make it happen.

So that is the first step: Repeat over and over again to yourself that you can make it happen. "Make it happen" is your new mantra for achieving any type of goal. If you find other inspiring phrases that grab you, use those to create a great attitude.

Many people in the business world consider General Electric's CEO, Jack Welch, as the best example of business leadership and accomplishment. Welch climbed the ladder to lead one of the world's most consistently successful corporations—not by luck, but by making it happen. A story in *Business Week* magazine cited Welch's "sheer force of personality, coupled with an unbridled passion for winning the game **No one is going to do it for you** of business." Welch came from a working class background, but rose to the top by seeking opportunity and changing the way his company did business to suit a changing market. Welch almost left GE after one year with the company due to the bureaucratic corporate culture there, so as CEO, he changed that culture and made the company even more successful than anyone dreamed. Only 12 years after joining the company, Welch wrote in his annual performance review that his goal was to be CEO —a bold statement but one that he made happen.

Making it happen applies not only to work and business, but also to your personal life. Several years ago, I was divorced with two kids, a single woman reentering the dating scene and looking for a really special man. I read that the only way to find your next significant other was to get out and meet lots of new people: take a class, go to an art gallery opening, go to parties even when you would rather stay home and eat ice cream. The perfect guy was not going to just knock on my door. I was going to have to go out and meet him wherever he happened to be. So I focused. I made it a priority to go out to new places and attend new activities. I increased my chances of meeting as many new people as possible. I went to a charity event one night—and ran into a man I had known in high school. I felt he might be the right guy for me, but it took a while before we were able to connect. One night I ran into him at the airport. I called him up, and we went out on our first date. Eventually I married Richard and started a new life with him and his children. While love sometimes seems a product of fate, it didn't "just happen." I had to make it happen.

A Good Attitude Creates Good Luck

Some people may think I am just lucky to have run my own business, published a book or married a great guy. But I don't believe in luck. You make your own luck. Many people say, "If I could only win the lottery, all my problems would be solved." Yes, you have to be lucky to buy the winning lottery ticket out of millions sold. But you definitely won't win unless you buy a ticket first. Winners make it happen by getting into the race.

Just like you won't meet the love of your life by sitting at home and dreaming about it, you won't make other positive changes unless you make them happen. If you want to find a better job, you have to get out there and make it happen step by step. The person who gets the great job isn't lucky; he has a positive attitude and focuses on the steps he needs to take to get that job. **You make** Instead of thinking about the steps you need to take **your own** to find a new job, you should be proactive, calling **luck** contacts (see Chapter Six on networking), searching the job listings, or going on informational interviews.

Not long ago, a woman I know named Janice found herself one of the many victims of the early 21st century economic downturn. An accountant with the giant agency Arthur Andersen, Janice lost her job when Andersen collapsed and folded. Although many of her laid-off colleagues went to work for Andersen's rival, Deloitte and Touche, Janice wanted something different. So she began searching for other job opportunities outside public accounting. She discovered a job opening in her hometown that sounded terrific, but after sending several resumés, she never heard from the company. Instead of giving up, Janice dug deeper. She found the name of a decision maker at the company and contacted him. She showed him a great attitude and a determination to get that job. He was so impressed by Janice's attitude that he helped her rewrite her resumé so that when the CEO of the company read it, he would hire her. Janice made her goal happen through hard work, resilience and creativity —as well as a positive attitude.

Your great attitude helps you take the actions necessary to find those "lucky" breaks. The only way to get through all the little steps you must take is by having that positive attitude. Stay focused on the end of the road and how great it will be once you achieve that goal. Don't waste time thinking about how successful other people are or how lucky these people seem to be. You will never get ahead if you misdirect your energy toward the negative: jealousy, worry, despair. Stay positive and stay focused on *your* goals. Your goals may be different from the next person's goals. Don't try to live up to someone else's standards or dreams. One person might want to be the CEO of a company, while you would be happy as the sales manager. What matters is finding what makes you happy and being sure of what you want before you go for it.

I know that I have the power to do what I want to do, and I keep my attitude positive, upbeat and energized no matter how challenging the goal may be. You can make it happen too, no matter what your goal. Use your great attitude to drive yourself from thinking to *acting on* your goals. Once you start the first action, the second, third and fourth actions will be that much easier.

Find what makes you happy

The Reward System

Many goals require a lot of steps to achieve, so you need to stay motivated. You must keep your attitude positive so you can focus your energy on the tasks you need to accomplish. I do this by something I call the "reward system." I reward myself for each step I take toward my goal. For example, I love reading for pleasure, but I won't let myself read a new novel or even the newspaper until I have spent time doing the things I *need* to do first. Reading becomes my reward instead of my escape or what I do to procrastinate instead of working.

I devised my reward system years ago when I wanted to confront my fear of public speaking. I was so nervous about making speeches that I couldn't eat or sleep for a week; I lost five pounds before every speech. So I realized that if I focused on preparing for my speeches well in advance, practicing and reviewing what I was going to say, I was far less nervous. Instead of procrastinating until right before the speech, which only increased my stress, I began allotting myself one to two hours a night—which I thought was manageable —of preparation. I knew that if I was very prepared, I would not be as nervous when I stepped up to the podium. If I stuck to my plan, I rewarded myself by reading a juicy new novel. Once I got started working on my speeches, and knowing that at the end of my work I would get my reward, I found that it wasn't so difficult after all. Often I worked even longer than the two hours because I got on a roll.

Reward yourself for each step you take toward your goal

Your reward can be anything you like: a manicure, a game of tennis, a movie night, or an afternoon on your boat. But you need to deprive yourself of the reward until you have completed some work on making your goals happen. Set up a schedule: Plan how many hours each week you need to work on your goal; decide what days you will put in those hours; and then pick the reward you will indulge in as your treat. Planning it—even writing it down on a chart or on your calendar—will help you stay focused. Be sure to reward yourself frequently; don't wait months before you reward yourself or you might give up! Create certain small rewards for work completed on a daily basis, and other larger rewards for goals accomplished on a weekly or monthly basis. Stay motivated by compensating yourself for work well done.

If your reward is something you love to do, it becomes even more enjoyable. It is no longer a guilty pleasure. It is your treat for putting in the extra effort. I used to feel guilty when I read for pleasure; I felt that I was wasting time when I should have been working. By making my pleasure reading a reward, I no longer felt guilty. I had completed my work, so then I could relax and enjoy a good book.

Rewards work well to motivate you to accomplish all kinds of goals. For example, let's say you really want to lose ten pounds and get in better physical shape. You know that you need to exercise at least three times a week to make it happen. So you review your calendar and pick out three times when you know you can get to the gym. As your reward, when you finish the third class of the week, rent yourself a copy of a hot new DVD and enjoy a movie night. When you make it happen, you deserve a reward, and those rewards will keep your attitude upbeat as you move toward your ultimate goal.

Even the world's biggest business leaders preach the

value of the reward system. General Electric's Jack Welch has said that he uses the reward system with his employees. When Welch was a young rising executive, the company practice was to offer set bonuses or raises, but when Welch became the leader, he changed that system to one of rewarding individuals based on the value of their particular accomplishments. Therefore, employees are more motivated and each employee knows that his or her particular achievements will be judged on their own merits. They are driven, and that's why GE continues to be successful.

Your goal won't happen unless you *make* it happen. You have the power to accomplish each small step along the way. If you have a positive attitude and **Rewards** stay focused on the ultimate destination, you will **motivate** get where you want to go. And those little rewards will keep you moving along the way.

Organization Smoothes The Way

Making it happen is easier if you are focused and organized. Most people (I am no exception) struggle to organize their lives and manage all the tasks they have to accomplish each week. Organization helps you prioritize what is most important. Organization helps you focus on the small steps you must take in order to reach your ultimate goal. A goal attained is simply a collection of smaller accomplishments crossed off your to-do list. As you cross each item off the list, you are closer to your goal.

I suggest that you make written or computerized lists of the important tasks you have to accomplish. Create daily to-do lists of things you must accomplish that day, and also create lists of larger, long-term goals. If you have a particular goal that is important to you—such as getting a new job, finding a new relationship or selling your house—take some time to slow down and analyze what steps you must take to accomplish that goal. Consider what is most important and what can wait. Focus on doing the important tasks so you can cross them off your list and move closer to your goal. There is no better feeling than the satisfaction that comes from viewing a to-do list with every item crossed off.

I take time at least once a week—Sunday night or first thing Monday morning is a great time to do this—and think carefully about what I have to do in the days ahead. I make lists and prioritize my activities and goals. I make two different lists: personal and business. All areas of my life are important to me, so I try to find ways to balance my time (you'll learn more about this in Chapter Ten) so I can achieve as much as possible.

Pick one night of the week and sit down for a few minutes. Choose a quiet place where you can be alone. Take a pen and a piece of paper (or buy a notebook, calendar or electronic organizer, if you like) and list what you must accomplish during the coming week. Review your to-do list along with your calendar and figure out what you have to do and when you have to do it.

Here is a good example. Your goal is to increase your fitness. You aim to do this by attending evening exercise classes at your gym three times next week. Review your calendar and determine which three nights work best with your schedule. On your to-do list, write "attend exercise class after work" on those three nights. In addition, note on the to-do list for the nights before those classes that you must "pack gym bag and place in trunk of car" so you can drive straight from work to the gym. By planning ahead, you make it easier to accomplish your task.

Organization and planning reduce procrastination because you can visualize what steps you must take and when you need to take them. Always review your to-do list with your calendar in hand so you know when you must do each task. Work backward from deadlines and determine at what point you must complete each step. If your goal is to sell your home and you wish to hold an open house for prospective buyers, create a to-do list of steps you must take in order to stage a successful event. If you have to place an ad in the real estate listings of the local newspaper, find out the paper's advertising deadline so you can submit the ad on time. Write "submit ad to newspaper by deadline date" on your to-do list. Days before the deadline, write "compose ad" on your to-do list so the ad is ready for submission and you have time to make changes if necessary. Complete the task and you can cross it off your list and move on to the next item.

Create Do-able Lists, Not Impossible Ones

Prioritize what you hope to achieve and focus on what is most important to you. Don't overload your list with every possible goal or you won't accomplish anything. You'll just feel overwhelmed and discouraged because you are not "doing it all." Concentrate on completing one or two important tasks at a time so you can devote the energy and time necessary to achieve them. As I've suggested, separate your business or career goals and your personal goals into two lists. Yes, it's important to create a road map for your success and plot out the points you must reach along the way to your goals—but make your goals manageable. Your day will seem much more successful if you create a realistic list that you can truly accomplish. Benjamin Franklin once said,

Planning reduces procrastination
"If we take care of the minutes, the years will take care of themselves." By creating to-do lists for each day, you manage your time more effectively. The small tasks you complete each day move you closer to your goal.

Planning and creating to-do lists improves your time management. You must not simply create a long to-do list. You must consider how long each step will take, when it must be done, what can be done simultaneously and what obstacles you can remove with smart planning (like gathering clothes the night before you need to drop them off at the laundry). We all have many things to do each day, so managing your time effectively is essential. As business guru Harvey Mackay says, "Manage your time or others will do it for you."

Let's say you have the following to-do list for a Saturday:

1. Buy new flowers and plant them in the front yard
2. Have oil changed in the car
3. Make pasta salad for a potluck party

4. Begin work on sales presentation for next week's meeting
5. Wash towels and sheets

The list contains only five tasks, yet poor planning could add unnecessary time to getting these tasks completed. The night before, plot out when and how you will do each task to make the most of your time.

Write that you should boil the pasta for your pasta salad the night before. Plan to get your oil changed early in the morning so you can beat the crowd. Write a reminder to bring your sales presentation files so you can read them while the mechanic is changing your oil. Plan to put your towels and sheets into the washing machine before you go outside to plant your beautiful new flowers. Schedule a break in your planting to stretch your legs (you don't want to be achy for your party that night). During this break, plan to pull your freshly washed laundry out of the washing machine and put it in the dryer. Write a **Create a** reminder to yourself that when you are done with **road map** planting and are about to get in the shower, you will toss the pasta you boiled the night before with prepared salad dressing. While you're in the shower and getting dressed, your pasta salad is marinating.

This is a pretty ambitious plan for a Saturday—most people won't cross every task off this list. And weekend lists will probably be quite different from weekday lists. But I'm trying to make a point: Think about what you could accomplish with a little advance planning. When you're done and ready to head out to the party, your sales presentation is started, your laundry is done, the pasta salad is prepared, and you can hop into your car knowing that the oil is changed and it's ready to drive.

Goals are really different from tasks. Tasks completed add up to a goal accomplished. When you make a to-do list, get in the habit of completing it.

I plan out each detail of what I have to do so I don't waste precious time on indecision later or find that I have forgotten an important step. When I go to sleep at night, I close my eyes and visually go through the next day's activities. What steps do I need to take, and in what order? I consider what I will wear, so that in the morning I can dress quickly and get out the door. I plan what I will need to take with me on my day's appointments. Do I need certain files or papers, or my insurance information, or a computer? If so, I think about where those things are located so I can easily grab them. I remember that before I leave for work, I should take something out of the freezer for dinner, and I think about whether or not I have plans to go out to lunch or if I should bring my lunch. If I know I have to be at work all day but I also have to go to the bank, I think about what point during the day I should get that task done.

Get in the habit of completing your list

On a daily and weekly basis, I make mental or written lists of both my goals and my tasks or "to-do" items. I check them and recheck them so I get things done. When it's time to chill, I can relax knowing that I have accomplished so much. If I have a list that I can easily refer to wherever I am—in the car, at work, at the mall, at a meeting—I move from task to task easily and don't waste my time. If you planned to go to the gym after work but forgot to put your workout clothes in your car, will you take the time to drive home, pick up your clothes and go to the gym? Maybe, if you are very dedicated. But most people, once they go home, will fink out and put off working out for another night. By planning ahead and writing a reminder to pack your clothes the night before and put them in your car, you remove that obstacle and accomplish your task. **Planning ahead is the first step**

Organization and advance planning make "making it happen" much easier. Try making simple lists at first and setting manageable goals. Keeping a "master list" on your computer is best if you have one, as a computerized file is easy to update. You can print copies to take with you,

"Your goals might be different from the next person's goals. Don't try to live up to someone else's standards or dreams."

as well as handwrite small lists on pieces of paper or in a pocket notebook for when you are on the go. Use the method that works for you. You don't have to be fancy or high-tech if that isn't your style—a mental list or a schedule scribbled on scratch paper works just fine. A combination of computerized and old-fashioned paper lists works best for me.

Planning ahead is the first step in making it happen. When you know where you are going and what small steps you plan to take to get there, the goal won't seem so out of reach.

- Are you a procrastinator? Why do you think you procrastinate?

- What small steps can you take now to begin the process of making your goals happen?

- What rewards will you use to help motivate you to take your first steps now?

- What methods can you use to plan your tasks in advance?

- When and where will you stop to do your advance planning, writing down what you want to do the next day?

- Do you have a mantra?

Never Take No for an Answer

If you don't like something change it.
If you can't change it change your attitude.

~ MAYA ANGELOU

SO YOU'VE SET YOUR GOALS AND REALIZED THAT you have to "make it happen." Even so, the next step won't be without twists, turns and occasional Wicked Witch problems.

Remember: Nothing really worth having or doing is easy. We always encounter roadblocks, but it is how you react to these roadblocks that will define the eventual outcome of your journey. Would Dorothy have made it to the Emerald City if she had given up the moment she encountered the Wicked Witch or her scary flying monkeys? No—she'd still be stuck in Oz, wandering around on the yellow brick road.

When you begin to "make it happen"—calling people about jobs, contacting banks about loans, asking people out for dates, or whatever it takes to get what you really want—occasionally you will encounter the **Nothing worth** dreaded "no." But when you hear someone say **having is easy** no, how will you react? Your response not only defines your eventual success, it also could change the immediate situation from a negative one to a positive one.

If you stop every time you hear the word no and develop a negative attitude about what you are doing, you will never get where you want to go. You'll stay right where you are—and if you're taking the time to read this book, we both know that isn't good enough for you.

So here's another mantra for you to focus on: Never take no for an answer. What I mean is that no doesn't always mean no in the world. Sometimes, it means possibly, or not right now, or I'm not sure, or give me more information to show me why I should say yes. The way you react to no is crucial. You can learn to revise your approach so it works better for both parties, to ease the no into a maybe and then, hopefully, into a yes.

I am not always able to get the perfect arrangement that suits my original vision, but I find that if I stay positive and flexible, I can get something pretty close to it, something that works for both parties. (Let me clarify one thing: When I say "no doesn't always mean no," I am not talking about relationships or sex. In those situations, when someone says no, she means no.)

Stop every time you have a negative attitude

Why Do People Say No?

If a person says no right off the bat when you ask for something, it doesn't always mean that the door is completely closed. People often say no as a protection mechanism. They may want you to offer them more evidence why they should say yes to your idea or proposal. They may be trying to make you prove your point. Or they may not fully understand how your idea will benefit them. People usually don't say yes just because you are enthusiastic or persistent, or because you think your idea is the greatest. Most people say yes only when the deal benefits them as well. Your job is to sell, sell, sell (see Chapter Nine) your idea (or your point of view, or even yourself) so they clearly see how it will benefit them to say yes instead of no. Your approach and attitude should be positive, encouraging others to be positive about your idea as well.

If you were asking someone to marry you, would you say, "Look, just say yes because I want you to"? Of course not! You would talk about the things you will achieve together, and how much stronger you will be as a team rather than as separate individuals. You would talk about all the happiness that "yes" will bring for *both of you*. It's no different in business or any other part of life, although there should be less kissing involved! When you want someone to hire you, invest in your business idea or accept an offer from you, you need to get that yes. *So get it.* Don't just take the no and accept it, sulk and move a step backward. If you took every no for a no, and didn't see the potential yes just on the other side of that no, then you wouldn't get anywhere.

Never take no for an answer

There is always a way to spin your idea differently to change no into yes. Know the person you are talking to. Try to understand everything about his or her desires and goals. Figure out what you have in common and how you can both benefit from working together. To prepare for any interview, proposal meeting, or even asking someone for a date, do your homework first, and do a little role-playing with a friend or even with yourself. Consider a few reasons why they might say no and come up with possible responses that you can use. Brainstorm possible alternatives you can offer, and practice having a positive attitude about the situation no matter what the outcome.

Listen to the Expert Inside You

Many people will give you advice along the way to your goal, and that advice may include, "No, don't do it. Stay where you are, where it's safe. Don't take that risk or you might fail." It's OK to take what they say into consideration, but don't necessarily believe that they are the ultimate authority. Don't let someone else's negative attitude affect your attitude and steer you away from achieving what you want.

Here's a great example of turning no into yes, from my own business experience. In 1990, I wanted to open a bookstore in Atlanta, my hometown. There seemed to be relatively few bookstores in a city that was growing rapidly to a population of three million, and I couldn't figure out why the major bookstore chains were ignoring this great market. I started off by doing some research in the book industry, and I called up three major book publishers to learn more. Their representatives told me that opening bookstores in the South was a waste of time because the South is illiterate. Naturally, I knew this was not the case! Two of these publishers told me not to do it—that I would be making a mistake. I didn't take no for an answer.

People say yes when it benefits them

(Ironically, when I was opening a children's clothing store a few years earlier, I heard similar discouraging words. The landlord of the shopping center told me that he had never seen a successful store of this type and tried to talk me out of it. My father also tried to discourage me, as he had been a clothing retailer and knew how hard it was. I did it anyway—and proved them wrong.)

What did I do? Sit around and complain about the ignorance of New York businessmen? No—I went to work. I conducted research on the successful track record of bookstores in cities similar to Atlanta. I learned that there was great potential that these New York-based publishers obviously were missing.

Atlanta was a city that attracted hundreds of thousands of educated, successful professionals and young families each year. I also knew first-hand that Southerners are not illiterate (I am one), and that all of my friends were avid readers. Yet there were very few bookstores to serve these customers' needs. I studied these existing bookstores and asked people what they liked and disliked about shopping there. I drew on my experience with Turtle's Music as well. Like the very successful Turtle's concept, I planned to open stores in neighborhood strip shopping centers, stores that all followed a uniform concept: bright, clean and organized so you could easily find what you needed. I wanted to emphasize customer service. While most bookstore owners were book lovers rather than business people, I approached the bookstore business with a seasoned retailer's eye. Plus, with my accounting background, I could read a balance sheet with the best. I felt that I could create a store that was different from the usual mom-and-pop bookstore and also different from the vast major chain stores.

If I had listened to the negative attitudes of these so-

Brainstorm possible alternatives

called industry experts, I may have given up on my idea before I began. I would never have opened my first store, Chapter 11 The Discount Bookstore, nor expanded to the successful, 13-store chain that my company became. I didn't listen to their no—I believed in my idea, I knew the South was not illiterate, I had a great attitude (because I trained myself to do so) and I made it happen despite the established odds against me. I didn't accept the current way of thinking because I knew in my heart that step by step I could "make it happen." I was afraid of failure, but this fear has always been one of my greatest motivators.

Step by step you can make it happen

When the Right Moment Comes, Act!

When I started in the bookstore business, I watched all the celebrities who came through town hold their book signings at another Atlanta store. These events attracted hundreds of customers and plenty of media attention, so I knew that it was important to have those celebrities come to Chapter 11 for their signings. But the publishers were used to sending their authors to the other store and often turned us down when we requested celebrity appearances. How could I turn those nos into yeses and get the celebrities to appear in our stores? I knew the right opportunity to change that trend would come, and when it did, I would be ready. My attitude was never discouraged—hearing no only made me more determined to make it happen the way I wanted it.

When I learned that Newt Gingrich, the controversial Speaker of the U.S. House of Representatives and a congressman from the Atlanta area, had a new book and was touring to promote it, I recognized a perfect opportunity to turn the string of nos into a yes. Gingrich was scheduled to speak at a rival store outside his district. I couldn't believe that the publisher had Gingrich signing books at a location outside his district when we had two stores that were in his district.

I had a great argument for a change of venue and decided to go for it. I used all my powers of persuasion to try to convince the publisher to move the location of Gingrich's signing, or ask him to do two events, which would have been a win-win situation for the publisher and a compromise I could live with. Nonetheless, the publisher again said no. I had to regroup and think about how to change the publishers' minds about our stores, how to convince them that working with us was actually in their best business interest. Again, I decided not to take no for an answer.

I did my homework, putting in long hours on a major presentation outlining the facts about our business, our standing in our community, and what kind of publicity and advertising we could promise for major book signings. I bound the presentation like a book and flew to New York to meet with the publicity and sales departments of all the major publishers. I came prepared with facts, but also with a winning attitude. My attitude told those publishers that I would not take no for an answer without pushing harder for common ground that worked for everyone, and that I would follow through and succeed on my goal.

to a no with dejection and a defeatist attitude, you will probably fail. If you react to a no with a positive, winning attitude, you will be more likely to carve out a deal that is close to what you want, or even convince the other person to say yes to everything you want. Nothing is set in stone. Don't take no for an answer without trying these strategies to finding a yes. They've worked for me and for many others; I think they'll work for you in almost any situation.

One: Get to the bottom of the no. Ask the person, "Why are you saying no?" Try to figure out how your proposal might be beneficial to both of you. See the other person's needs and think about how **React to a no** your idea might serve them. For example, if **with a positive,** you want to sell a company a new product, **winning attitude** think about how your product might help their business run more efficiently. Consider that they may not realize that their current equipment doesn't do everything it could for their business, or that your equipment could save them money in the long run. Write a few of these points.

Two: Put it in a different way. Think about how you may be able to rephrase your request to make it seem more appealing to the other person based on his or her needs. Let's say you are trying to buy a car from someone at a lower price than advertised. Ask the person, "Wouldn't you like to sell this car and have the money in hand? I am ready to close this deal and give you a down payment now." Come up with some solid reasons why the person should consider your request further. Keep the conversation going. Think about how you can create a scenario that is a "win-win". Respect the other person's needs and intelligence—you have to bring a great attitude and a great proposal to the table to get a yes!

Three: Consider a compromise. Even if you get repeated nos, it's important to keep the lines of communication open. Propose a compromise. Let's say you are trying to convince a local TV personality to chair the fundraising carnival at your children's school, only she has said no. Ask her, "Would you consider at least signing some photos or merchandise to auction at the event, or putting in a good word with some of the others at your station so we can find someone else?" You may be able to get something close to what you want even if you don't score the big victory right up front. You also establish a relationship with the person that can lead to more cooperation in the future.

Don't let yourself become huffy or openly disappointed when a person says no. It's better to have a partially open door than one that is permanently slammed shut because you were unwilling to compromise. Stay calm. Present your case without getting excited or confrontational. Always be on your best behavior because nice people come across as decent and honest—and they are usually rewarded in the end. Build a relationship.

Four: Wait and watch for a better opportunity. Just like my bookstore and the celebrity autographings, sometimes you have to be patient and wait for the right opportunity to get what you want. Sometimes no isn't final. Sometimes people change their minds, and their situations may change to make them more willing to consider your idea. Nothing stays the same in business or in life. What seems written in stone today may be erasable tomorrow! Be willing to give it time so you can prepare more information, and keep an eye on the situation so you know when it is right to ask again. People are often impressed by persistence, and will give you a chance because they see that you are really determined to make it happen.

Five: Don't be discouraged—no matter what! It's important to maintain a great attitude even if you don't get anything out of a situation. Let the other person see that you are positive and enthusiastic. Your reputation is incredibly important. If other people see that you can remain positive in the face of defeat, they will respect you and speak highly of you. In the future, things may change, and they will be more likely to come back to you if they had a positive experience dealing with you.

Sometimes, No Means No

Of course, sometimes no really does mean no—and in those cases, you have to figure out what steps to take next. Just because you hit a real roadblock in your quest—a loan that doesn't come through, a bankruptcy, a failed business, being laid off from your job—doesn't mean that you will never reach your goal. It just means that you may have to get there a different way.

Here's a personal story that was very troubling at the time, but turned out OK in the end. Late one night a few years ago, I received a call from my then-teenage daughter. It was every mother's nightmare: She had been arrested and taken to jail. I said, "Let me talk to the officer." Knowing that I never take no for an answer, I tried to talk to the policeman and convince him that there had to be other options than taking my daughter to jail. I tried every trick in my book to convince him to change this course of action, but I could not do it. His answer

Get there a different way

was no. My daughter didn't let this one error of her youth become a permanent detour on her road to her goals. She's now on her way to a successful art career, and we can recall the one time when we had to deal with a no that we couldn't turn into a yes.

This may be an extreme example, but you have to learn to accept some roadblocks and find a different road to your dream. Like the example of my daughter, one mistake didn't destroy her whole life. We stayed positive and used this episode to learn an important lesson. All things happen for a reason, and you must make the best of each situation—even bad ones like this—and maintain a good attitude. I was fired from my job and learned lessons about what I really wanted to do in my career. Bernard Marcus was fired from his job and went on to co-found The Home Depot, one of the largest corporations in the world.

Usually, you can find a way to make things work for everyone, including yourself. But you must be realistic. Not everything is possible. With a winning attitude, you can find compromises and, step by step, work toward your ultimate goals of a more satisfying life.

Never let one no get you down. Nobody—even movie stars or CEOs of major corporations—rises to the top of their field without at least one failure or hearing one no. In fact, it's likely that all successful people have heard many nos on their way to the top. The difference is that they don't accept the rejection as final. They seek a variety of possible opportunities (a tactic I call "putting lots of irons in the fire") and explore many ways to achieve their goals. That's what you should do too.

Each situation you encounter prepares you better for the next situation. If you receive a no that doesn't turn into a yes, at least you have learned a great deal about the process. You've learned where **Find a different** there might be flaws in your proposal, or that **road to your** you may be asking the wrong person. Let's say **dream** you get turned down for a promotion you sought. Step back and think about where you can go next. Is there another job or another company that might be a better fit for you? Is there a better way to approach others about your ideas? Can you get help from other people to refine your efforts and find the path that works?

Bad things sometimes happen for good reasons, and the obstacles you encounter can spur you to work harder and achieve your dreams. As famed football coach Lou Holtz once said, "Show me someone who has done something worthwhile, and I'll show you someone who has overcome adversity." Hearing a no doesn't mean that your effort is hopeless. It just means that you must find another way to get the job done. Most of the world's most famous, successful people faced obstacles—even outright rejection—and went on to triumph. Elvis Presley auditioned for a record producer early in his career and was told not to give up his truck driving job. General Douglas MacArthur had to apply to West Point three times before being accepted. As a young student, Lucille Ball was told by a drama instructor to try any other profession except performing. Successful novelists Anne Rice and Stephen King both had to endure extreme poverty while trying to publish their first books, enduring many rejections from publishers who felt nobody would want to read novels about the supernatural.

Is there a better way?

Imagine how different things would be if any of those people had heard no and just given up.

Don't give up on your ultimate goal. Your attitude will take you there, even if you must take a lot of small steps to get there. Remember, Dorothy didn't fly right in to see the wizard. She had to take a lot of steps on the yellow brick road to get there. She needed to go through many trials and errors, and find the right allies to help her in her quest. She had to endure some rejections from the wizard and jump through a few hoops that he placed in her way. But she knew that if she was going to get out of Oz and get back home, she had to make it happen. She found the courage not to take no for an answer, even from a wizard. She was persistent and maintained a great attitude, and that took her where she wanted to go.

You can do the same thing by not taking no for an answer. No is simply a signal that you have to work harder, keep trying and stay positive. Your attitude should always be focused on the possible, not on the impossible. Having that upbeat attitude will be the fuel that carries you to what you really want in life. **Don't give up**

- What is your usual reaction when people say no? Do you think you can react differently having read the suggestions in this chapter?

- How can you prepare better for a situation so you react more positively when you hear a no? What is realistic for you?

- How can your idea or proposal be a "win-win"? How will you describe it to the person you are approaching?

- How can you better negotiate to get what you want? Are you willing to compromise?

Everything Is an
Opportunity

There are only 3 colors, 10 digits
and 7 notes, it's what you do
with them that's important.

~ RUTH ROSS

AS YOU'RE STROLLING DOWN THE YELLOW BRICK road, you may find, as Dorothy did, the occasional fork. You should view these forks as opportunities – and you will have to choose which opportunity you will pursue and which ones you will pass by. But remember: No matter what each piece of road looks like on a map, everything is an opportunity.

You'll come to dozens of forks as you travel down the road of your life—in your career, your love life, your family life, your personal growth—and you should view every opportunity as something worthwhile to consider pursuing. You should never focus only on one opportunity. What if it doesn't pan out? You'll feel discouraged and won't know where to turn next. Dorothy had focused solely on the wizard as her way out of

Keep many irons in the fire

Oz, but when his hot air balloon left without her, she found that she had other, better options. Glinda the Good Witch, with whom she had a good working relationship, offered her a more direct, less dangerous route.

Your attitude should always be positive. Your outlook should always be wide open to a multitude of possibilities. Great opportunities don't always knock on the front door. Sometimes they sneak up on you. A golden opportunity may not look that great at first, but as you do your research, you may find that it's just right for your needs. You must be open-minded to see the opportunities that benefit you and take you where you want to go.

This approach is what's known as having lots of irons in the fire, a concept I mentioned in the last chapter. I make it a point to always have many irons in the fire, simultaneously pursuing several potential opportunities to increase my odds of moving forward. Send out lots of resumés, not just one or two. Apply for positions you may not think you want just to learn more about them and how your skills fit in different companies. This tactic applies to your social life too. If you're in the dating world, don't just focus on one venue for meeting people—go to many different types of events, explore the Internet or volunteer in your community to increase the pool of potential dates you can encounter. Develop a network of friends you can make plans with every weekend, so you're not always depending on one particular friend all the time. Having lots of irons in the fire increases your opportunities for success and keeps your attitude positive. If one opportunity doesn't pan out, you have many others to pursue. You can always move on to the next challenge instead of constantly looking backward, trying to figure out what went wrong.

Be Willing to Look and Listen

Just recently, I was in a meeting for a company where I work as a consultant. The president and other executives of the company were in attendance. In the meeting, someone asked us, "Are you in the market to make acquisitions, because we have something you might be interested in." The company's president answered quickly: "No." She went on to explain her decision: The company was focusing on sales and profitability, not expansion and investment. I immediately jumped into the discussion. In a positive tone that didn't undermine the president, I said, "We will be happy to take a look." A look is free. Listening to a proposal, considering an option and reviewing a possibility takes nothing more than a little bit of your time. You never know when the perfect opportunity will come your way or what you may learn from the experience. *Everything is an opportunity.* Always keep your competitive edge in any situation. If you are going to find that uncut diamond waiting to be plucked from the dirt and polished into treasure, you must always be looking. If you aren't looking, you won't find anything, and life's great opportunities will pass you by.

It's true that you won't be able to pursue everything. Nobody can do everything they dream about doing, or take on every opportunity they encounter. Sometimes you have to choose. But your attitude should be that if everything is an opportunity, then it is well worth your time to listen and consider any proposal. Even a fork in the road that seems barren now might be filled with good fortune tomorrow, so take a little time to investigate the possibilities and consider them seriously. Don't just say, "I don't have time to consider that now. I'm pretty happy doing what I'm doing now. It's not a great time to change. Maybe in a year or so, I'll want to think about trying something new."

My daughter is really happy with her job. But recently, someone called her about another opportunity. Although she was content in her current position, she went on an interview. She didn't take it, but the experience made her feel even more positive about the job she has. She didn't turn down the opportunity to listen just because she is satisfied. She took the time to find out more so she could determine whether or not this would be an even better opportunity. This is networking. The more people you talk to and the more possible ventures you explore, the greater your chances of finding the best opportunities.

In a year or so, a lot could change—for the worse or the better. In fact, the opportunity you are "too busy" to consider today could turn out to be a gold mine a year from now. The comfortable, pleasant situation **Expand** you are in today could turn out to be a losing **your circle** proposition a year from now. You might say, "I wish I had looked at that opportunity a year ago…I wouldn't be stuck in this mess now. I just had no idea things could change so quickly."

Don't be caught flat-footed when it's time to run. Always look around at opportunities to improve your life and situation. Always be willing to listen to someone else's ideas if they come to you. Always be willing to grab a cup of coffee or have lunch with someone who may be a great contact or a new friend. Expanding your knowledge and your circle of acquaintances can only increase your chances of being ready to jump when the great opportunity comes your way.

Consider New Approaches

I learned that everything is an opportunity when I owned the bookstore chain. Eight years into our business, we had grown steadily by opening 12 stores from scratch. We were successful and had built a great reputation in our community and industry. But we thought there was only one way to grow—by finding new areas of town where bookstores didn't exist, renting space and starting a new store. We had never considered acquiring an existing bookstore whose owner wanted to sell.

I was sitting in my office one day when the phone rang. It was a man who owned a bookstore in Gainesville, a large town about an hour north of Atlanta. This man wanted to sell his store to our growing chain.

My first instinct might have been, "We don't buy existing stores; we create our own. That's our business model." But I believe that everything is an opportunity, and this acquisition might be worth a look. I met with my staff and told them that we were going to Gainesville to look at the store for sale.

They all thought I was crazy and was wasting my time. We were in the business of opening stores from scratch, not in buying existing stores. But I told them that we should at least take a look at the store and see if it was worth buying. I thought we may be able to learn something from this man or from his store, and learn more about the bookstore market in this region. Remember: Looking is free, except for your time, of course. I felt this was worth my time.

We drove up to Gainesville and I knew I wanted to buy the store at first glance. It was big and beautiful, almost twice the size of our other stores. Unlike our other stores, this place sold both books and music, and that prospect excited me, as I had previously been in the music business with Turtle's. I was hoping I could afford to buy this man's business and turn it into a new outlet for our chain.

He was asking a pretty steep price. I took the package of financials back to my office and began to review them, to see if the store was worth his asking price. His price was too high, but I wanted the store. I knew I had to make it happen.

I did some research, asking more questions. My homework paid off; I learned that he wanted to sell out urgently because he wanted to be free to pursue another opportunity. He didn't have the time or the desire to spend running this business as it should be run. As a result, he was not doing a good job and I felt that there was potential for success with the right leadership. Selling the store to us would make this man look like a winner, at any price, because nobody would know how much he had made or lost. Once I learned these facts, I knew his reputation could not be counted in dollars.

With this information in my mind, I made a low offer to see how he would react. He accepted! I realized that he wanted to sell this store very badly. Obviously, he simply wanted to sell and had asked a much-too-high price to begin with to see if he could get it, but was willing to accept our lower offer.

We made a great acquisition and added this beautiful store to our network at a fantastic price. It was a win-win situation. This man sold his business with his reputation intact and we bought a great store for a price that would benefit us greatly. But I would never have made this terrific addition to our business had I not been willing to take a chance, think outside the parameters of my normal practice, and drive an hour to take a look at what he had to offer. I took a chance to review an opportunity despite the fact that my staff said it was crazy and a waste of time, and it turned out to be a winner.

Be Ready to Negotiate

In the last chapter, I talked a little bit about the art of negotiating a "no." Every opportunity is an opportunity to negotiate for better terms. Very little is written in stone. You can change the terms of any situation by clever negotiation. You have to be willing to take a chance and you also must be willing to walk away if the negotiations don't pan out. I love to negotiate—it's an exciting game.

Be willing to take a chance

The economy, a person's financial situation and timing are always key factors when you are negotiating. The man who was selling the store was willing to negotiate because he wanted to unload his business to pursue another opportunity. A friend of mine always goes to buy a new car on Christmas Eve, because the salesmen are more eager to complete the sale and get home to their families and make their quota—they're more willing to give this friend generous terms on the sale.

The price of an item is almost always open for negotiation, particularly when you are dealing with the person who owns the store. When I was traveling with a friend in Hong Kong a few years ago, I spotted a piece of jewelry in a store. It was beautiful, but the price was more than I was willing to spend. Instead of just walking away discouraged, I contacted the store owner when I returned to my hotel room and said, "If you're willing to sell me this piece of jewelry at my price, I will give you my credit card right this minute over the phone." I told him what I was willing to pay for the jewelry, a 35 percent discount off the retail price. The jeweler told me he would call me right back. He obviously thought about it, and felt that a sale in hand was worth more than waiting **Bring your** around for someone to buy the piece at the higher **own terms** price he wanted to receive. He called me right back and took the order. I had my jewelry—at my price and on my terms. While this tactic may not always work, it's important to keep in mind that you can try. Everything is an opportunity to get what you want on your terms. Don't just conform to other people's needs or terms just because they're on the table—bring your own terms to the discussion.

Always keep in mind that you should negotiate from a position of strength. Negotiate for better salary or terms when your business is strongest or when you have just finished a project and did an outstanding job. Increase your chances of getting what you want by showing that you stand on firm ground and have many other opportunities at hand.

Keep Those Irons in the Fire

Remember: Every opportunity you explore won't turn out to be that perfect opportunity. You have to be willing to take some chances, and you have to use your best judgment when deciding what to pursue and what to pass up.

To increase your odds of finding a great opportunity, you need to put yourself in a good position to encounter as many opportunities as possible. You must have lots of potential opportunities cooking all at once.

Even if I feel like I am riding high, enjoying a great job or business situation, I always keep my eyes and ears open to new opportunities. I send out resumés and apply for interesting positions (even if it's something I haven't done before). I have lunch with new people who may lead to other contacts and connections, I ask lots of questions. I keep adding new people to my circle of acquaintances and business colleagues. I go to parties, events, lectures and volunteer meetings. Why spend my **Put yourself** free time looking for something new when what I **in a good** have now is just fine? Because you don't know **position** when things can change. You might begin to feel bored with your current situation and want to find something more challenging. A downturn in the economy might affect your company's business and make your job less enjoyable or lucrative, leading you to seek change. Or, you could find something that is even better than the terrific situation you're in now—there is always room for improvement, believe me! When I first started exercising to get in better shape, I started with small goals like running a 5K race. Soon, I was running 10Ks, and then half-marathons. Eventually, I began competing in duathlons, something I never dreamed of doing. You never know in what direction that first small step will take you.

Even when business opportunities don't pan out, I

keep my attitude positive and focus on the next opportunity. Even a great opportunity isn't the only opportunity you can pursue. Usually, things happen for a reason, and they happen for the best, so keep your eyes and ears open to lots of possibilities.

Keeping lots of irons in the fire helps you reduce or even avoid that feeling of rejection that we all hate. It can apply to any situation. Let's think about jobs. If you're looking for a new job, would you just apply to one job, even if it's the perfect position for your needs? That's not a great idea—if you pin all of your hope on getting that job and the offer doesn't come through, you will feel discouraged, even deflated. It's better to apply to several jobs, increasing your odds of getting an offer or multiple offers. That puts you in a better position to negotiate for the best terms. If you already have a job, it's easier to find a better job because you are negotiating from a position of strength.

In dating, every new activity is an opportunity to meet someone special. If you pin all of your hopes on one singles party or football tailgating party, and don't explore other venues for meeting people, you decrease your chances of meeting the right person. Often, a single person will meet someone and immediately decide this is "the one." That's natural—but is it wise? If you focus only on one person and exclude others, you could be setting yourself up for disappointment. You're better off trying to meet a number of new people, going out on lots of casual dates for coffee or lunch until you know for sure the person you like best is really "the one." By keeping your options open, you are meeting new friends and contacts. And you might discover that someone you may have passed up is really terrific for you.

The irons in the fire technique works for any situation: even babysitters. When my kids were little, if I wanted to go out with my husband, I had to find a babysitter. Anybody who has children knows this is a big challenge! Good, reliable babysitters are hard to find, and everyone is trying to get their services, particularly on Saturday nights. So I didn't just pick one babysitter to use—I had a list of at least five sitters that I could call on. That way, I had a better chance of finding someone who was available. I hated the feeling when I called one and she would tell me she was busy, but I knew that I could call on several others to find someone to help me out.

If you have lots of possible opportunities to fall back on, then rejection stings less.

Hey, if getting rejected by a babysitter bothered me, you can understand why I always have lots of irons in the fire. This technique is key to attitude. Achieving and maintaining a great attitude requires action on your part—it isn't just some magic thing that you put on, like a pair of ruby slippers. I do everything possible to keep my attitude up and feeling good. I create an environment in which I am improving my chances of getting what I want and going where I want to go.

Listen, we're all human. Rejection stings. It can dampen some of that positive attitude that you've worked so hard to build. But if you have lots of possible opportunities to fall back on, then rejection stings less.

You can just move on to the next possibly great opportunity. In the case of my babysitters, I'd just call the next one on the list. I raised my chances of getting what I needed.

Set Yourself Up for Success

When your attitude is optimistic, you increase your chances of success. A recent study conducted by the Georgia Institute of Technology showed that people— even those who have lost their jobs or been laid off— have more success finding one if they are optimistic and view their previous job loss **Create a positive** as an opportunity to improve their situa- **environment** tion. The study showed that a person's attitude, their psychological approach, was a vital factor in the success of their job hunt, as much as their resumé or qualifications.

Recently I sold my business. I wasn't sure what I wanted to do next. Some people in my situation might have wanted to take some time to relax, reflect on past accomplishments, travel or try a new hobby. I wanted to get to the next challenge—that's how I keep my attitude high. Although for years I had focused on owning and running a company, I felt that ending this phase of my life was an opportunity to embrace an even more exciting challenge.

The next step wasn't immediately clear, so I started making opportunities happen. I called a headhunter—a professional who specializes in linking qualified people to jobs—and interviewed for lots of interesting positions. Again, I didn't stick to what I had done before, but searched for new roles that might challenge me and help me grow. I looked at businesses for sale that I might invest in or buy. While I was doing this, I started to write this book. I had never written a book before, but I had read so many of them. I felt that I had something to add to the discussion of how to go where you really want to go. Even though I had never written a book before, I saw it as a new challenge and a great potential opportunity.

Although writing a book was a big project, I focused on pursuing other opportunities at the same time. I didn't want to set myself up for failure or disappointment if one project didn't turn out to be successful. If other people see that you have many irons in the fire, you will seem more desirable. People will offer you the choicest opportunities because they know you are in a position of strength.

Attitude is a vital factor in success

Now that I have sold my bookstore chain, I am involved in a variety of new, exciting roles. I consult, speak to groups around the country, I'm involved in a real estate business, I'm a board member of different businesses and non-profit organizations, and I also teach business students at a local university. In the meantime, I'm looking for more opportunities that may be just right for my talents. I have interviewed for many jobs, exploring new and interesting fields. I'm not satisfied with the status quo—everything is an opportunity that leads to something better.

You never know what twists and turns life will bring. Sometimes, careers end and you can either find new opportunities or flounder. Just because one pursuit ends doesn't mean you can't do something completely different and find success. Wayne Rogers, the popular TV actor who starred as Trapper John on "M*A*S*H*" for many years, became a successful financial analyst and mutual fund manager as his acting career waned. Now he appears often on financial TV programs, offering his expertise on economic issues. In 1984, Vanessa Williams became the first African-American winner of the Miss America pageant, but her reign ended abruptly when "Penthouse" magazine unearthed and published nude photos she had posed for earlier. Instead of crumbling after the disgrace, Williams focused on her talents as a singer and actress. She worked hard, pursued performing opportunities, and became a major star. In the end, Vanessa Williams found greater fame than most Miss America winners who kept their crowns.

Go Ahead and Ask the Question

Sometimes, you have to put an iron in a fire that you didn't even realize was lit. Great opportunities may be hard to recognize—unless you ask about them. I used to own a publishing company, and there's an interesting story about how I found this investment opportunity.

One day, I was sitting in my office when the phone rang. It was a guy I knew from the book business, the head of sales and marketing for a publishing company we often bought books from. He asked me, "Barbara, would you read a manuscript for a new book we're thinking about publishing?" I agreed to do it. I don't always get a chance to read everything that people ask me to read, but this manuscript intrigued me. The book was called *The*

Jewish Phenomenon. I'm Jewish and therefore, I wanted to find out what the Jewish phenomenon was, at least according to this writer. So I took the manuscript home with me and read it in bed that night. I loved the book and thought it would be a great success.

Great opportunties may be hard to recognize

The next morning I called the sales and marketing guy back to tell him how much I loved this book. I told him, "I think this book is going to make the *New York Times* best-seller list." I didn't just want to see this book become successful, I really wanted to be a part of it. But how?

I felt that this book might be a potential opportunity for me. I said to the guy, "Hey, do you need a partner?" He said, "Hold on a minute." Then I heard him get up and close the door to his office, so I knew something good was coming when he got back on the phone. He picked up the receiver again and said, "Coincidentally, I'm in the process of trying to buy this company from the owners. So I do need a partner."

Originally, he thought he could buy the company on his own and leverage the purchase. But he found that he could use a partner like me. So since we love to "make it happen," that's just what we did. We made the purchase of this company happen. First, we tried to understand the current owners' psyche: Why did they want to sell the company? We put ourselves in their shoes. We figured out that they were a part of a huge company, but this was a tiny division that they had hoped to grow, but it never happened. In a nutshell, it was like buying the bookstore.

The owner really wanted out at this point, so we made a great offer that was a win-win situation for both sides. If I had never looked at this as an opportunity, and never asked the question, I would have never owned a publishing company. I had no idea the business was for sale and that I could get in on the deal—but I searched for the opportunity that was hidden there.

Owning a publishing company was a great challenge and full of excitement. Two years later, I wound up selling my part of the business back to my partner, but not before we took another book to the *New York Times* best-seller list, which is the book industry's **Look for** version of winning an *Oscar*. So keeping multiple **opportunties** irons in the fire led me to a growth opportunity, expanded my experience in business, and gave me the thrill of publishing a best-seller.

So don't just let opportunities come to you. Look for

"If other people see that you have many irons in the fire, you will seem more desirable."

them, even in places where they are not obvious. Be bold enough to ask some questions about possible opportunities that may be there for you to capitalize on. Realize that everything you encounter is a possible opportunity— and have a positive attitude that tells other people you are in the market for something special.

- What opportunities do you want to seek right now? What are some first, small steps you can take now to make them happen?

- What opportunities have you passed on in the past? Why did you let these opportunities slip by? What could you have done differently?

- How could you negotiate from a position of strength the next time you buy a car? Apply for a loan? Ask for a favor?

- Do you usually have lots of irons in the fire or do you focus on one opportunity at a time? Why or why not? What could you do differently to maximize your potential return?

Just Ask

If there is something to gain and nothing
to lose, by asking, by all means ask.

~ W. CLEMENT STOWE

JUST ASK. THIS IS ONE OF MY FAVORITE MOTTOS. Many times throughout my life and career, I have been willing to just ask for what I really wanted, even if it seemed far-fetched. Why not just ask for it? You never know when someone will surprise you and say yes.

How did Dorothy, the Scarecrow, the Tin Man and the Cowardly Lion finally get what they wanted? They overcame their fear of the thundering, intimidating Wizard and just asked for what they needed: a heart, some courage, a brain and a way to get home. In the end, the Wizard was not that intimidating (he was a little guy hiding behind a curtain) and he was willing to help them find what they wanted. If they had been afraid to ask, they would have stalled. And you will stall too – unless you just ask.

Don't be afraid of rejection

Most people are afraid to just ask because they are afraid of potential rejection. They set themselves up for failure with this attitude; they visualize the negative reaction rather than the person saying yes. Yes, rejection hurts. But it is a necessary step in the road to getting what you want, as we discussed in Chapter Three. Other people may be afraid to just ask because they feel they are being pushy or grasping for too much. I agree that it's important to be realistic about what you ask for, but don't worry about appearing pushy if you are going for something you truly want or need. Chances are good that if you don't just ask, someone else will come along without that fear and will get the very thing you want – the great job, the date with the fabulous guy down the hall, the discount on the car.

Go Ahead, Give It a Shot

When you go for something you really want, people will often tell you that you're nuts. I've heard it plenty of times. They'll say that you are aiming too high. They'll say you have no chance because the opportunity isn't there. They'll tell you that you should look elsewhere. But if you really focus on what you want, and stay positive about the possibilities that are out there, you will find the courage to ask for what you want. You will see the possibilities that other people may overlook.

The first business I started from scratch was a children's clothing store called Bubble Gum. We used to **Aim high** give all the kids who came in the store a piece of bubble gum, so they always wanted to shop with us and dragged their parents to our business. As the mother of two little girls, I felt that I knew what clothing moms like me were looking for. I felt that I could present this merchandise in a better way than the existing stores were

> ### "You miss 100 percent of the shots you never take."
>
> ~ WAYNE GRETZKY

doing. In addition, I felt that this type of store would allow me to continue my business career and still be a hands-on mother to my daughters. This career move gave me the flexibility I needed to work in the business world and raise my children.

I started by researching the market for children's clothing. I had a hard time finding clothing for my own children that was both fashionable and reasonably priced. I researched possible locations for a retail store, and came up with a solid business plan and marketing strategy. The first thing I knew I would need was a loan. Before I went to the bank to apply for a loan, I discussed my approach with my father, who has always been my business mentor. He felt I was asking for too much. "The bank will never give you that much money," he said. Maybe I was a bit naïve, but I thought, "Why not just ask?"

So I did. I felt that the worst thing that could happen was that the bank would tell me no. If that happened, I would rework the request until it worked and I got the money I needed to start the business. Or I would go to another bank. I just asked, but I also backed up my request with solid facts and a business and marketing plan.

I walked in with a positive attitude and just asked for the amount of money that I knew I needed. I presented my excellent business plan, supported by my knowledge of accounting and finance, and an innovative marketing plan. To the utter surprise of the people who had told me I was crazy, the bank's loan officers said yes. I had to be flexible – they asked me to put up a bit more collateral than I had originally planned. But I had my loan and I could start my business. The important point is that I did my homework, and just asked for what I wanted…and the bank's loan officer didn't laugh at me. I believe that my attitude about my business concept won the day. My father was amazed – astonished, in fact. I was

What's the worst thing that can happen?

thrilled and ready to sell the best children's clothing at the best prices in town.

There would be another obstacle to overcome. The landlord of the shopping center where I wanted to rent space didn't want to rent his vacant spot to a children's clothing store. He believed that these stores were never successful. I had to convince him, and sell **Do something** him on the idea that my approach would be a **different** winner. I did a *great* sales pitch to this man. I convinced him that I was going to do something different with this store. Small boutiques in town sold fashionable clothes at very expensive prices. The department stores sold more affordable clothes that had no style. I decided to feature fashionable merchandise at affordable prices. Nobody in town was doing this, and I was con-

"Don't be afraid to ask if someone tells you no—remember never take no for an answer."

vinced that I could make it happen. I knew that it was important to give the customers something different, not just by discounting (which I did), but also by stressing customer service and marketing my attitude. (See more on the art of great salesmanship in Chapter Nine.)

He realized that if I could convince him, I could sell my children's clothing and attract customers. This approach also convinced the bank to give me the loan I needed to get the business off the ground. My attitude and solid business plan made me successful in the end.

You Never Know When They Will Say Yes

Attitude is key to getting what you want, because when you have a positive attitude about your goals, other people sense it and react seriously to your requests. If you have a negative attitude, you ask for things with less confidence. People react with skepticism. If you don't believe in your idea, how will other people buy into it? Don't be discouraged before you even start asking. There is always the possibility that the answer will be yes, so believe in that possibility. Feed your attitude with a positive spirit.

People will sense your confidence

Years ago, I purchased a station wagon from one of the biggest car dealerships in town. I was prepared when I walked onto the lot, negotiated well and was very proud of the deal I received on the car purchase. Shortly afterward, I was talking to my friend Barbara, and she told me that she had just bought the exact same car—same model, year and features—for $2,000 less than I paid. I was stunned. Not to be deterred, I contacted the general manager of the dealership where I had bought my car and told him the story. I asked to receive the same price that my friend had received. The general manager listened to my pitch, and told me he would discuss it with his staff. Soon, I received a $2,000 check in the mail from the dealer.

When it came to my business loan, I really believed I could get the money I was after. In this case, my inexperience worked to my advantage. I prepared as much data as I could to back up my proposal. And I believed strongly in my business idea. Your attitude and belief in yourself will provide the winning edge, but you must also be realistic. Don't ask for something that is impossible; stretching for something slightly out of reach is more realistic. If you do your research, you'll learn what is realistic and possible. Twenty years ago, how many people thought that millions of people worldwide would pay $2.50 for a cup of gourmet coffee? Most people would have laughed at the suggestion, but Starbucks is a huge success today because so many people are willing to do so every day. Bottled water is another great example. Technically, most bottled water is no different than what comes out of your tap, but many companies market this product with flair and people will pay several dollars a bottle for something they could drink for free.

After I had been in the book business for a few years, I decided to plan a sales retreat to educate my staff and to reward them with a good time. But my company couldn't afford to pay for what I wanted to do. So I decided to ask the publishers – the companies who supplied the goods that we sold in our stores – to pay for the retreat. This seemed pretty bold and innovative. **Inexperience** Nobody had thought about asking for something **can be an** like this before. I didn't think about the publish- **advantage** ers saying no or laughing at my idea. I concentrated on how to make it happen.

I developed a strategy and a presentation that would get me what I wanted—a retreat for my employees—and also serve the publishers' needs. Just asking is more than "the ask". You have to do the work to prepare for "the ask" so you can back it up. When you ask for something, people will want to know how it benefits their needs. You have to prepare to tell them how your innovative idea is really a win-win opportunity.

I told the publishers the retreat would be an opportunity for their companies' sales representatives to pitch their new books to our employees. The store employees are the ones who actually sell the books to the customers—they're a key link in the chain between manufacturer and end-user. If the publishers could convince my store employees that their books were the ones our customers had to read, they'd see big sales as a result. By helping me pay for the retreat, they were making an investment in their own sales. I presented the idea as a win-win situation for all of us.

Put in the time and effort

It worked. The publishers saw the opportunity and were willing to grab it, even though it was something totally new to them. The retreat, known as our "Fall Festival," became a much-anticipated annual event that both my employees and the publishers looked forward to. We enjoyed ourselves and increased our business at the same time. The publishing companies not only paid for the costs of our retreat, but they also brought truckloads of free books for the store employees who attended. My employees, who were all book lovers, enjoyed getting the first look at the hot new books coming out in the future season.

Do Your Homework—It Pays Off

I've mentioned several times that you have to do your homework before you just ask, and before you can make it happen. You must be prepared when you ask for something. Of course, sometimes you have to be spontaneous and jump on an opportunity. But you should be ready to put in the time and effort to research an idea, put together a thorough and solid proposal, and make it look and sound polished.

Doing your homework also means asking questions and thinking about what the other person may need. If you're going to just ask, you increase your chances of getting a yes by putting in the time to prepare your argument and back-up plan. If you're going to just ask, you increase your chances of getting a yes by presenting a win-win scenario to the other person. You also increase your chances of getting a yes if you think creatively instead of imagining just one possible scenario.

When I was in the bookstore business, we almost lost an opportunity to host the best-selling author David Guterson for a signing in our store of his new novel. Guterson had written "Snow Falling on Cedars," a hugely popular bestseller that was **Do the** being turned into a movie, and his new book **research** was sure to be a big seller, too. I wanted him to **necessary to** appear in our store, not in one of our rivals. But **secure the yes** the publisher was looking for a venue that had a large seating space, so the author could read to an audience. Our stores were smaller and didn't have large seating areas like some of our competitors did.

Did we give up? Are you kidding? No—we just asked. We not only asked for Guterson's signing, we thought creatively. Since he wanted an auditorium and we didn't have one, we looked for one we could borrow. We did some homework and eventually found a local college that would allow us to use their auditorium for free. They wanted the prestigious author to appear at their school. They were small enough that they didn't have their own bookstore on campus to compete with us, so they didn't care who sold the books. We got the event and the sales by co-sponsoring the event with the college.

Ask for some-thing a bit crazy

It was a big success. The author loved the college atmosphere, and hundreds of people from the community came to hear him read and bought his new book. The college even had some money in their budget that they had to spend before the end of the semester, so they paid for catered food and flowers! All we had to do was ask, but we did the research necessary to secure the yes. In the future, we used this approach to attract other celebrities who wanted to speak to an audience, including Dr. Phil McGraw, Harold Kushner and Suze Orman.

Be a Creative Negotiator

Sometimes you just ask for something that seems a bit crazy. Other people may think you will do more harm than good by asking for it, but if you believe there is a good chance you will get what you really want, you should be willing to go for it.

Recently I discovered that the payroll company we were using for our business had made a mistake. The mistake was not easy to prove—sort of a "we said/they said" situation. I know I gave them the right information, but I could see how they may have misunderstood it. It was hard to prove that the mistake that cost our company money was really the payroll company's fault, but I thought, "How can I make it work to benefit our business?"

I realized that the payroll company didn't want to lose our business. Instead of behaving in a confrontational manner—which often gets you nowhere fast—I decided to be a creative negotiator. This is very important—keep your cool. I didn't push the blame for the situation in their face. I simply found another way to recoup those dollars. I proposed that since they had made a crucial mistake, they should offer us 12 months of free services. My accounting department thought I was crazy, that the payroll company would never agree to this proposal. But the company did agree. They knew the mistake could have been their fault and that the other options were either losing our business, ruining their reputation or even facing litigation (although we wouldn't have done that). They decided to keep a customer happy—and this customer used that to her advantage. I have found that when you're asking for something, it can be easier to get services or discounts instead of money, so keep that in mind.

Keep your cool

When it comes to looking for a new job, you always have to just ask. Opportunities are not always posted on the Internet or in the want ads. Sometimes the perfect job for you doesn't even exist—you have to creatively negotiate for it. You network (see Chapter Six) to find the right people at the right companies that suit your interests. If the perfect position isn't open, propose your services to the company—perhaps on a temporary basis, or even as an outsourced employee. Companies are more willing to take a risk on hiring someone if they don't have to immediately pay for benefits or retirement accounts. Once you show them what you can do for their bottom line, you're uniquely positioned to get the great, permanent job.

Show what you can do for their bottom line
As we learned in the last chapter, when you are trying to buy something, don't assume the price on the tag is the final price. Would you pay the sticker price for a new car? Then why take this approach with anything else? Almost everything is open to some creative negotiation. Recently I was on vacation with a close friend. One day we were out shopping when I found earrings in a jewelry store on one side of the island. I loved the earrings, and I asked for a discount, but the store said no. I bought the earrings anyway. Well, I should have followed my own advice and

"Almost everything is open to some creative negotiation."

held out for what I really wanted. Later, when my friend and I were shopping together, we went into another branch of the same store on the other side of the island, and my friend spotted another pair of earrings. She asked the store for a discount and they agreed. I decided to call the store owner and insist that I get a discount too, since his store was willing to give someone else a break.

You've heard this a million times, but it's important:

Be proactive. Ask for what you want. Don't wait around for someone to call you if you really want to talk to him or her about an opportunity—or even a date.

My favorite "just ask" success story involves a dating tale. As I told you briefly in Chapter Two, I knew my husband, Richard, from my high school youth organization days. Many years later, we were both single parents, and I ran into him at a charity event. I wanted to go out on a date with him, but he never called me. I thought, "Why shouldn't I just call him?" While conventional wisdom said that the woman should wait for the man to call, I decided to just ask. When I first started dating again after my divorce, my girlfriends told me that if a guy asked you out for Sunday night, you shouldn't go, because it meant that he had something better on Friday and Saturday nights, and that you were number three on his list.

Don't listen to the rules

I worked up my best confident attitude and called him up to see if he'd like to get together. He said, "Sure—how about Sunday night?" Despite the conventional wisdom, I went on the Sunday night date. One date turned into a great relationship. We fell in love and got married. So don't listen to the rules if you really want something to happen—just ask.

- What keeps you from asking for what you really want?

- How could you better prepare for a situation in which you are asking for something? What homework could you do beforehand to increase your chances of success?

- Are you afraid of rejection? What steps can you take to overcome your fears?

- Can you recall any of your own experiences when you have been a creative negotiator with success? What worked and why? Can you apply this to other situations? How?

Six Degrees of Separation... or Networking

"You can make more friends in two months by becoming really interested in other people than you can in two years by trying to get other people interested in you. Which is another way of saying that the way to make a friend is to be one."

~ DALE CARNEGIE

SUCCESSFUL NETWORKING IS THE KEY TO GETTING almost anything you want in life. Who you know can be as important to your success as what you know. You've heard this many times, but I am here to tell you that it is true. I live by the power of networking. Great opportunities, rewards and people don't just knock on your door—you must go out there and find them.

How did Dorothy, a frightened young girl stranded in a strange land, survive all those dangerous challenges and find her way back home? She networked. She met the Scarecrow and made him her friend and traveling companion. Then she saved the Tin Man and convinced him that joining her group was the way to get the heart he so badly wanted. Later she brought the Lion **You are never far** into the fold, too. In a short period of time, **from reaching the** Dorothy went from stranded loner to the **person you need** ringleader of a tight, cooperative team. They worked together to get to the Emerald City and to defeat the Wicked Witch of the West.

Talent is not always your greatest asset in today's economy. Beauty is not always your greatest asset in today's social world. But knowing the right people is a key asset to getting ahead. There is a famous play and movie, "Six Degrees of Separation," that purports that every person in the world is connected by six acquaintances or fewer. I don't know if this is true, but the idea is very powerful. You are never very far from reaching the person you need to contact if you just work the network of friends, colleagues and relatives you already possess.

There are many intelligent, talented people toiling in

unsatisfying jobs because they don't know how to network their way into a better position. But knowing lots of people is just the beginning of networking – you must also learn how to work those contacts and use them to your best advantage.

Networking Wherever and Whenever

Networking has helped me in every aspect of my life. In business, I network constantly and hear about everything, including job openings and other opportunities, that most people never discover. Networking allows you to get the scoop on the latest news, party invitations, hot dates—even a table at a restaurant. Having the inside track in almost any situation is

Knowing lots of people is just the beginning

really not about money. It's about knowing more people than the next person, and being someone that lots of people know.

Just the other night, my girlfriend and I walked into a popular restaurant for dinner. It was packed—the host told us we would not get a table for two hours. My girlfriend's response was, "Let's go," but before we left, she went to the ladies' room. In the two minutes I was waiting for her, I spotted the head waiter. I knew the man, talked to him, and in another two minutes we had a table. In this very simple case, making a contact and using it later when I needed it got me what I wanted. It put me at the top of a long list.

I've always made a point to be very involved in everything that interests me. The more I do, the more people I meet and the more knowledge I gain about every situation. There is no shortage of interesting things to be involved in—not just work, but also social clubs, professional groups, sports, new friends, politics, theater, everything. You just have to decide what you like and how you wish to spend your free time. Don't do anything you don't like, but don't stay home either. Make yourself get out and do something at least once a month. When you have small children, this can seem like a challenge, but there are activities where you can involve your whole family, too. You might also investigate activities you can do while your kids are in school, or ask your husband or wife to take care of the kids during this one night.

If you're like me, you won't want to restrict yourself to activities just once a month—you'll want to do things at least twice a week. Start with once a month and then expand your horizons so you don't feel over-

Don't stay home

whelmed. It's a little like exercise (which we'll discuss more in Chapter Eleven); you may hate it at first, but after you make it happen, it gets better every minute. Networking expands your mind: by meeting new people and getting involved in new activities, your understanding of the world around you and its possibilities grow. You discover new opportunities that you never knew existed.

Harvey Mackay writes in his book *Dig Your Well Before You're Thirsty* about how, after graduating from the University of Minnesota, he struggled to earn a living as an envelope salesman. His father suggested that he use the one thing he was truly passionate about—playing golf—to help him network his way into a better career. His dad told Mackay to contact the head of a local golf club and convince the man that he, a skilled golfer, would be a great asset to the club, which had consistently fielded last-place teams in citywide golf tournaments. In exchange for Mackay's golfing talent, he asked the club to waive the membership fees, which he couldn't afford. Mackay had nothing to lose—and the club accepted the deal.

Of course, the real reason Mackay's father had pushed him to join the club was the unlimited network of influential businessmen he could meet there. Mackay subsequently was able to meet the **Utilize your** right people at the club and make the contacts **family network** necessary to rise in his business career. Without putting himself in the right networking circle, Mackay may have never gained access to the best opportunities. But he pushed himself into that networking circle through sheer will (and a low handicap).

In this case, Mackay's first networking contact was his father, who cared about him enough to offer him a great idea. Utilize your family network when you need advice, ideas, connections or referrals. Make the occasional one-on-one lunch date with a cousin or a retired uncle. Reach out to your parents' friends or longtime neighbors. Often, these people care about you and will be glad to offer a contact at a local company or a piece of useful advice. They're also very skilled at fixing up people on dates. I know many people who met the loves of their lives after being set up by an older relative or family friend.

So What Do You Like to Do?

Networking opportunities can be anything: softball league, book club, quilting bee, painting class, investment seminar, exercise class, neighborhood association meeting, church committee, local political campaigns.

Put yourself in the right networking circles

Networking opportunities don't have to be organized affairs, nor do they have to entail a lengthy time commitment. You can decide to ask one new friend or colleague to lunch each month. Networking is just talking to someone new, and gathering information about the world they live in to see what opportunities exist for you. And it's fun!

Many people are nervous about the unknown. Doing new things is easier with a friend, so if you can ask a friend or your spouse to join you, take someone along.

I was greatly interested in politics, so this became one of the first extracurricular activities I pursued. In the early '70s, I attended a fundraising dinner for a charity and found myself seated next to a man who was running for Mayor of Atlanta. We talked during dinner and I found that I really liked him. He impressed me, so I, always looking for an opportunity, told him I'd like to work on his campaign.

I qualified my interest by telling him up front that I had a full-time business to run, so I could give only a few hours a week. I also informed him that I was a CPA, and would be interested in working in a financial role. The very next day, he sent me a telegram asking me to be the assistant treasurer for the campaign. (Later I realized that he was also taking advantage of "everything's an opportunity" by pursuing me as a volunteer. I had approached him about working on his campaign, but he recognized the opportunity to gain a skilled volunteer and followed up on it, and that shows why he was a successful politician.)

I was flattered but also nervous. I knew it was an opportunity I couldn't turn down, but was I biting off more than I could chew? Somehow, I figured I would make it happen. And I did. In the **Network** process, I had a great time, learned many new **with a friend** skills, and met tons of people who helped me in later projects and business opportunities. To make it all worthwhile, my candidate won—Maynard Jackson became the mayor of Atlanta as well as a leading figure in national politics. He also became a valuable addition to my network. After his recent death, the city honored him by renaming its massive airport Hartsfield-Jackson International Airport.

One place many people turn for networking is their professional society or association. Most professions have these associations, whether your field is sales, public relations, accounting, truck driving or air-conditioning repair. Sometimes these are unions that are usually locally based but may be connected to national organizations. Here you have a natural connection to the people you meet. You work in the same field, so if you're looking for specific opportunities, you'll find people who can give you educated opinions and leads. However, these are also your competitors for customers and jobs. It's worthwhile to get involved in associations in your profession, but the real networking happens when you expand your horizons. Try something totally new, and you'll find out so much more about the possibilities for you and your career.

Find New Challenges by Networking

You never know what new, exciting challenges await you just by networking. You might encounter an opportunity to do something you never imagined doing. Recently I was interviewed on a cable television show by a local reporter. I was curious about this woman's occupation—how did she wind up working in television? **Document who you meet** Instead of remaining curious, I asked her to meet me for lunch one day. I asked her questions about her job and the field of television. I used my new information and old contacts to pursue this exciting idea, and within months I was asked to host a local cable show about Israel. I would never have encountered this opportunity to work in television and expand my job experience if I had not taken the action of calling this woman and asking her to meet me for lunch. I made a new contact and followed up on that contact. I was open to new challenges, so the sponsors sought me out. Opportunities find you only if you look for them!

Stay in touch with your contacts and constantly update your contact information. You can do this the old-fashioned way, by listing everyone you know in a Rolodex or an address book, or you can take advantage of the new technology available on the Internet. E-mail makes staying in touch easy, and most programs allow you to conveniently save and update contact information so it is at your fingertips when you need it. Contact important people or friends periodically to check in, set up a coffee or lunch date, or ask for advice. If you call people only when you need a favor, you are not really networking. It's important to e-mail or call people just to maintain the relationship, so when you need their help they will be there for you. I keep business cards of people I meet, as well as the new cards of friends when they change jobs or businesses. Often I write a few notes on the back of the card to remind me later of the different affiliations or skills these people have. When I meet someone new and take out their business card weeks or months later, these notes help me remember the person, where I met them, and how they may be able to help me.

You never know when networking can result in a great opportunity. The connection can yield a result months or even years later. Lou Holtz, the famous **Stay in touch** former head coach of the University of Notre Dame football team and currently head coach of the University of South Carolina, once told how he landed his first football job at Ohio State University. For years, he kept up with a single person he knew who worked on the coaching staff there, calling the man periodically just to say hello. Finally, when there was an opening, Holtz was fresh on the contact's mind. He interviewed and won the plum job, and later went on to a great career in football.

Try Helping Someone and You'll Help Yourself

Charity/volunteer work is an easy way to network. Many people who volunteer outside their jobs do so because they have a personal commitment to improving their communities and promoting a good cause. There's no pay involved, so these are not lazy people. They're often smart, successful people who are willing to put in extra hours to make a difference. And since they're not competing with others for business or promotions, they're very open to talking to you about opportunities. Find a cause that speaks to your heart, whether it's helping children with cancer, supporting an important political cause or raising money to improve the environment in your community. Every group is always looking for volunteers.

I joined one local organization as a volunteer and met another volunteer who was the owner and publisher of a magazine. I was very interested in her career, and she was interested in mine. Three months after I met her, the magazine did a three-page story about me. Today I'm a consultant for her publishing company, which has expanded from the one magazine to four. My involvement with this successful, growing company happened because I signed up to volunteer for something I believed in and met someone new. Meeting that one new person opened an exciting career avenue for me, but I never would have found this new opportunity without networking.

Networking isn't just about jobs or business opportu-

Volunteer outside your job

nities. It's also about finding new friendships and even romance. If you're single and out of school, you may wonder how you go about meeting potential dates. Going to bars to meet new people isn't always an appealing idea, and you probably won't wish to go alone. But volunteer work can be a great way to meet new friends and potential dates. You can get to know people in a more relaxed setting where you can be yourself. When you make new friends, they can introduce you to a whole new set of people and activities. Many churches, synagogues, community centers and apartment complexes also have singles groups where you can meet other single people for sporting events, parties, trips and other activities, no matter what your age.

Don't Wait for the Phone to Ring—Dial It Yourself

Networking is most successful when it is a two-way street. Dale Carnegie said that the best way to have a friend is to be a friend. Keep up with your network and be there to listen or offer a good lead when your friends need help, and those people will be there for you. Be willing to meet someone who just moved to town for lunch or coffee. Offer yourself as a reference if a friend or relative asks you to do so, as long as you feel confident in the person's abilities. Call a contact of your own to make a referral for another friend who needs the connection. Those people will be there when you need a referral, contact or lead.

When you move to a new city, networking to meet new friends is so important. My friends Andrea and Mike are one of the most popular couples in Atlanta. They are involved in community leadership roles and are seen at almost every social event. They became socially successful despite the fact that they uprooted their life and moved to a new city. When they came to Atlanta, instead of hanging out at home, they made a strong effort to go out, sign up for volunteer work, attend events, and make social plans with the new people they met. They didn't let people come to them—they went out there and met everyone they could meet. This is brilliant networking. I know other people who have lived in a new city for years and say that they haven't met a soul, and that they're bored, lonely and discouraged. They have no one to blame but themselves. They need to get out there and network.

If you like sports or outdoor activities, networking is easy. You don't have to be a great athlete to participate—there are leagues and groups for people at almost every level (even totally clumsy!). Many sports leagues are more social than competitive and give you the chance to get some exercise while meeting new people. In addition, check out clubs that do hiking, biking, rafting, canoeing, walking or other outdoor activities. I have enjoyed participating in tennis, golf, runs, biking events, and active group vacations, and have met many new and interesting people in these activities. Most of these clubs welcome people of different ages and levels of fitness. Check out the web sites of companies that organize trips involving outdoor activities, where you can meet new people and explore new locations.

If you have never done anything outdoorsy or athletic, why not take lessons in tennis or golf, or even join a neighborhood walking club? You'd be surprised at how far you can progress and how many new people you can meet. You don't have to get involved in an expensive, organized activity. It's as simple as meeting a few people for a game of bowling, or asking some friends at work to go for a walk after **Great opportunities** hours. Or even organize a group to try a **don't just happen** new restaurant for a weeknight dinner once a month. These outings give you the chance to talk outside your normal environment and routine—and that's when real networking takes place.

How to Make Networking Happen

Networking is a bit of a subtle art. At best, it should be natural, but there are methods you can use to network more successfully and get what you want from these new conversations and experiences. It's important to enjoy yourself, relax and have natural conversations, but if you really want to network successfully, you have to know when to ask questions and when to work your new contacts to your advantage.

First, don't forget that great opportunities don't just happen. You make them happen. Getting off the couch and going to new activities is the first step. What do you do then? Here is where you put your positive attitude to work.

1. **Smile.** I like people. I'm always smiling, so I appear approachable. That's exactly what I want. I want people to be drawn to my positive attitude and to feel that they can come up to me, meet me and begin talking to me. Body language is very important. Hold your head up, stand up straight and look people in the eye so others feel that you are open to meeting people.

2. **Create dialogue.** Be genuinely interested in what the other person is saying. If you can't do this, then pretend! It's important to be engaged in the conversation, so you can ask important questions and find out information that you may need to know about this person. If you can, find out what important or interesting people will be attending a party or event before you go. With the new Internet E-Vites, you can often see who is on the invitation list for an event and who has accepted. Otherwise, just ask around. Always be prepared as much as you can to create engaging conversation. Read the newspaper or current books and magazines. By being well-read, especially good periodicals like the *New York Times* or the *Wall Street Journal*, you will always have something interesting to add to any social conversation. This makes you seem informed, and it also helps create interesting dialogue.

3. **Look your best.** How do you feel when you have on your favorite outfit? What does it do to your attitude? You probably feel like you can take on any challenge when you are wearing that power suit. So

clean out your closet now, and throw away everything that does not make you feel like you do in your best outfit. A black suit is the most important thing you own, so buy the best that you can afford. Wear the jacket on the weekend with a white T-shirt and you'll feel like a million dollars. For men, a black suit and white shirt and a great tie suggest confidence and style. No matter what your current physical shape or size, you can look well put together. When you're going to network, wear clean, attractive, appropriate attire. If you're unsure about what is appropriate to wear to a certain event, call up the organizers and ask beforehand, or ask some friends what they would wear. Be comfortable but be appropriate. Think about how you appear to others in what you are wearing. If you can, ask a good friend to tell you honestly how certain outfits flatter you. Most department stores also have free wardrobe specialists who can help you find clothing that suits you and is appropriate for various occasions. If you're a woman, you probably wear make-up, but you must learn to apply make-up properly. Department store cosmetic counters offer free consulting and demonstration services—take advantage of these services and find out what looks best on you.

4. **Be willing to approach others.** Although I appear approachable, I also like to make the approach most of the time. I don't wait to be approached. I look around for someone not engaged in conversation. I seek out people who look

like they want to meet someone new and I approach them. I introduce myself and start asking lots of questions. I'm looking for a common denominator between us. I usually start with, "What do you do? Where do you work?" If this line of conversation is a dead end, I find out where they are from or where they live now. You can always find something in common to talk about. It's rare that I don't find a connection with someone, but when I don't, I say it was nice to meet you and move on to someone else.

5. **Take a friend with you—but don't stick to them like glue.** It can be tough to walk into a room full of new people when you're alone. So take a friend with you, or even your husband or wife. You'll feel more comfortable and confident knowing you have someone to talk to and someone to leave with. But networking involves meeting new people, so don't stick to your friends or the people you already know and forget to meet others. Make a pact with your companion to separate for a period of time—say 30 minutes—and try to meet new people. Plan to meet up again at a certain place and time so you have an anchor to rely on. This technique also allows you to compare notes. Your friend may have been talking to someone whom you should meet, someone with the perfect job contact or someone you would be interested in dating. You can also offer your friend information about the people you've met. It's like tag-team networking; you accomplish twice as much!

6. **Make the most of every opportunity, but don't lock yourself in.** Some networking opportunities are a bust. You have to be willing to take some chances where networking is concerned. You may find yourself stuck in a dead-end conversation or attending an event that seems to offer little opportunity to network. View every situation as an opportunity to learn something new or meet someone new. In volunteer activities or job networking, you never know whom you will meet and where. Enjoy talking to new people, but don't lock yourself in if you can help it. Make sure that you mingle and meet more than one person at events. Don't stand in the corner and talk to your friends or co-workers. Meet someone new. Be willing to try new activities so you are not always going to the same events and

> **"The more I do, the more people I meet the more knowledge I gain about every situation."**

encountering the same people. Stretch yourself, and you'll gain so much more.

7. **Bring business cards or something to write on.** If you have business cards, make sure you always have a few with you to give people you meet. It's easier for someone to contact you if they have your card with your title, phone number and email address printed on it. If you are not currently work-

ing, consider getting cards printed that have your contact information. These can cost as little as $10 for a large package. Most printing shops and office supply stores have business card printing services.

If you prefer organizing information electronically, record the information of people you meet on your cellular phone or PDA. As I said earlier, take the person's business card and record the information in your computer or Rolodex later on. If you find yourself without a card or if they don't have one, always make sure you have a pen and a small pad to write on. You'll find it easier to contact someone later if you can get his or her phone or email information, rather than trying to look them up in the phone book or on the Internet. Write a few things about the person you meet on the back of his or her business card. Months after meeting someone, I can pull out a business card, see the notes I have written on the back, and make the connection. I can call that person, remind him or her about our meeting, and then we are reconnected.

8. **Follow up.** When you meet new people that you'd like to talk to further—whether for business or romance—make sure you follow up with him or her promptly. Don't wait three months to call or email someone that you just met. They may not even remember who you are! Contact them within a few days or a week at most. Send people emails or forward emails that seem interesting to people you'd like to keep up with. Then they will remember

you. Set up lunch or an after-work cup of coffee. Schedule an informational interview if you'd like to learn more about their profession or business. Most people are glad to talk to someone new about what they do. By making the move yourself, you don't have to wait around hoping that someone will contact you and produce an opportunity. You're in control. They'll appreciate your confidence and you'll find networking a much easier, more productive activity.

- Do you enjoy meeting new people or does this make you nervous? How can you overcome your nervousness about meeting someone new?

- What keeps you from trying new networking activities? Is it your schedule, your husband or wife, your kids or your job? Are there networking activities that better suit your schedule and your needs?

- When you go to a new event, do you walk around the room and meet new people, or stand in one place talking to someone you already know? How can you change this habit? What barriers stand in your way that you could overcome?

- When you meet new people, do you contact them or wait for them to contact you? How long do you wait to contact people after you meet them? Do you think you could set a time limit for yourself to try to set up a meeting with someone you've met?

Focus, Focus, Focus

The greatest discovery of my
generation is that a man can alter his
life simply by altering his attitude

~ JAMES ADAMS

NO MATTER WHAT YOU WANT TO DO OR WHERE YOU want to go, once you have started your journey, you must focus, focus, focus on your goal. Do not let yourself lose focus of your objective. People who maintain their focus act more efficiently and effectively, and often get what they want because they are always aware when opportunities pop up.

Imagine if Dorothy had started skipping down the yellow brick road and then, in the middle of her trip, had lost her focus. She might have ended up flipping pancakes in some backwoods Oz diner instead of conquering the Wicked Witch and taking the Emerald City by storm. Dorothy may not have had a college degree and a flashy wardrobe, but she was very focused. She wanted to see the wizard and get back to Kansas, and she never let anyone (least of all, herself) forget that.

What does it really mean to focus? To concentrate. You have to concentrate on the task at hand, so you can put all of your great attitude and energy to work.

Concentrate on the task at hand That's how you do a great job and get the results you really want. When you focus, you follow through on your plan and check important items off your to-do list, instead of coming back to that list months later only to find that you've made no progress at all.

Most importantly, you must focus on what you really want. We talked about this in Chapter Two—you have to know what you want to do in order to make it happen. Otherwise, you're just wandering around an endless yellow brick road that leads to nowhere. You need to focus on what's really important to you so you can set priorities. This is called maximizing your efforts – you want to get the maximum result for the effort you put forth so you don't waste time and energy.

Don't Worry About Everyone Else—Focus on You

My daughter called me recently to tell me that her boss had come into her cubicle to discuss something important, something that others in the office should not hear. My daughter was concerned because she felt that everyone could hear what she and her boss were saying, and she was so worried about her co-workers' reactions that she wasn't really focused on the important conversation at hand.

I told her not to worry. Chances are that no one was listening to her conversation with her boss, because everyone was focused on what they were doing. I have an office, not a cubicle, but through the walls I can hear every word the salesman in the next office says. But I have never listened to a word he has said. Why? Because when I am at work, I'm so focused on what I am doing that I might hear sounds but I don't hear words. I don't have time to take my mind off what I'm doing long enough to actually listen to what someone else is talking about that doesn't concern me. Of course, my daughter's co-workers may have been eavesdropping on her conversation, but if they were, they probably weren't successful at their own work. Successful people are focused on their work, not on office politics and snooping on their colleagues.

Don't worry about what other people are thinking about you. That's a distraction and a waste of your time and energy. Focus on what you're doing so you can do it as effectively as possible.

Focusing is not always easy. You may have to train yourself to focus if it is not something you do naturally. But you can learn by continuing to remind yourself what you are trying to accomplish, both for the short term and in the long run. Many people clutter their minds with unimportant thoughts that distract them from focusing on their important goals. They may worry about why the guy they met last weekend hasn't called them yet. They may be concerned that a co-worker doesn't like them. They may think about the exercise that they used to do but don't anymore. Instead of worrying about these things, why not focus on proactive ways to accomplish what you want? Get to the heart of your passions and goals and find actions that can help you achieve them. Maintain a positive attitude and a solid focus in order to get where you want to go.

Don't worry what other people think

This is another instance where simple planning and organization can make a big impact. Take some time each day—maybe as you are traveling to work or on your way home, or even for five minutes as you start your day over a cup of coffee—to think about what you need to accomplish. Make a short list for that day. This list can be mental, written on paper or typed on your computer. You might even leave yourself a voice mail message. Think about how what you do today can lead to what you eventually hope to accomplish. It's important to focus on what you are doing at the moment, but it's also essential to remind yourself periodically why you are doing all of these small tasks: to reach your ultimate goal. Dorothy had to focus on getting through the challenging tasks that faced her on the yellow brick road. If she had lost her focus, she would never have escaped the flying monkeys and defeated the Wicked Witch. She maintained her focus on her ultimate goal: to see the wizard and get back home. That's why she was successful in the end.

Get to the heart of your goals

Try the Three-Things-at-Once Method

How did I learn to focus? Well, I've worked for myself for 25 years, so I have always had some flexibility of when I could leave the office. For some people, this kind of flexibility would make it difficult to focus—they need structure and boundaries. But I set my own structure and boundaries so I can accomplish what is necessary within a time schedule that I've set for myself. I have become my toughest boss and won't let myself miss my deadlines.

When I'm in an office setting, if someone walks into my space to ask a question or seek advice, I totally focus on him or her. But once our discussion is completed and any issues resolved, I immediately turn my focus back to my project at hand.

Nevertheless, I don't like focusing on one thing for very long. I find that I lose my mental edge if I work on the same project for too long. Bored people don't accomplish very much, even if they have plenty of time on their hands. So if you find yourself becoming bored, find something new to focus on—even something simple like cleaning out your closet. Activities, useful projects and creative thinking can stimulate your drive and help you regain focus and passion for your dreams.

I combat mental boredom by working on about three things at once. I do a little work on one goal and then move to the next, make a phone call, go back to the first task, and so on throughout the day. That way, I accomplish a great deal but never get bored.

Most people today have a lot on their plate, so you probably know what I mean about having multiple things to do at once. The good news is that your creativity level goes up when you have more than one thing to accomplish. If you are focusing on one task and find yourself in a rut, switching to another task for a while can help you think of solutions. Shifting your focus to something else relieves your frustration with the stalled project and, often, helps you find great ideas to solve the problem. When I was working in accounting and couldn't make a balance sheet work out, I knew that if I stepped away from the troubling task—maybe going to lunch and not thinking about it for a short period of time—it would make more sense when I came back to it.

Find some-thing new

Set the Right Goals for Your Dreams

As I said earlier, it's important to focus on what you really want to achieve and to define the goals that will make you happy. Don't focus on trying to achieve something that is really someone else's goal, or you won't be satisfied in the end. We all have pressure from people in our lives – parents, spouses, friends – to do certain things, but the most important person to listen to is you. Your focus should be on what you will do to make yourself happy, not to make your mother, spouse or boss happy.

Here are a few tips to help you focus on your goal and how you will achieve it.

First, search your feelings and try to clarify what you really want. Try to be as detailed and focused as possible when defining that goal. Your goal should not be vague, like "I want to make a lot of money." Your goal should be specific and have value. Search your soul to focus on why you want to make a lot of money, and what you are willing to trade off (long hours at a job, for example) to achieve it. It is important to set attainable goals. If you are now an administrative assistant at a small company, it may be unrealistic to set a goal of being a CEO in five years. Set goals which improve your life in manageable steps. If you're now an assistant, setting a goal to be on the accounts receivable staff may be more realistic. Once you achieve that goal, you can focus on your next step.

Secondly, be patient. Clarifying your goals may take time, even months. You may have to overcome many distractions – family, kids, financial struggles, your job – to achieve the focus necessary to make and maintain change. Don't be impatient. Be willing to take some time to focus on your goal and to tinker with the details until you get them right. Be willing to change your goal as you absorb more knowledge and learn what is realistic to achieve. It's better to take five years to focus your life's lens on the exact goal you want to achieve than to grab the first opportunity that comes along – only to wind up disappointed. There are many setbacks in life, but you must be willing to maintain your focus and plow through these challenges if you are going to achieve your goals in the end.

Thirdly, focus on specific, small steps toward the ultimate goal. If your goal is to make money, include the method you will use to achieve financial success, such as the particular career path you will take, the companies you would like to work for, the investment strategy you will employ, or the type of business you would like to start. If you don't define the steps you will take to move toward your goal, you probably won't get very far down the yellow brick road. Goals should be realistic, and should include small steps that lead toward the ultimate goal. An example of an ultimate goal is "to marry someone wonderful." Examples of small steps to reach that goal are "join online dating service and log on at least once a week" or "go to at least one new social occasion each month to meet new people." Those small, manageable steps can add up to a very big goal! And you will feel as if you are doing something positive to reach that goal, rather than sitting around feeling that the goal is unattainable.

Finally, step back once in a while to focus on the bigger picture. Don't allow yourself to only focus on one goal at the expense of everything else in your life. Yes, it does take a lot of energy to achieve something great. It takes a lot of time and effort to achieve a goal like getting a new job, finding a new love or writing your first book. Don't focus all of your energy, time and attention on only one thing and deprive the other important people and pursuits in your life – particularly your family – of the nourishment they need. You may not be able to do it all, but you can do quite a lot if you stay organized and focused on the really important things in life.

Stay Organized to Stay Focused

I always keep a to-do list. We talked about this earlier, but I think it's worth reemphasizing. Organization keeps you focused on your priorities and helps you get things done so you can move forward. That **Organization** sounds really simple, but I think it's essential. It **keeps you** doesn't matter if you use a notepad or an elec- **focused** tronic device, or scribble notes on the back of your supermarket receipts and stick them in your purse. Recording a to-do list for each day helps you stay focused, organized and efficient.

I use a to-do list so that I never have those frustrating moments where I don't know what to do next. Boredom is poisonous to a positive attitude. When I finish one project or the three at once I am working on, I cross off the completed tasks and immediately start working on the next thing on the list. Crossing items off my to-do list gives me a great deal of satisfaction and a sense of accomplishment.

If you are in a position where you're not really busy,

do something about it now. The busier you are and the more challenging your activities are, the more you will accomplish each day. Think about the days when you are so busy you hardly have time to look at the clock. At the end of the day, you say to yourself, "I can't believe what I did today!" Often, instead of feeling drained, you feel energized and proud of what you have been able to achieve by staying focused.

Now, think about those days that you don't have much to do. Maybe you wake up on a sunny Saturday and find that you don't have plans for the day. You could do so many things, but you get lazy and wind up doing nothing. I am not saying that you shouldn't have these lazy days (they can be reinvigorating), but the busier you are, the more you will accomplish. On those Saturdays when you are active and get a lot of things on your list done (like shopping for new shoes, exercising, pruning the trees in the yard, or visiting your best friend whom you don't see as often as you'd like), you feel great at the end of the day. So stay active and be a person who has a busy schedule. You will move ahead on your list of important things to accomplish in life if you focus, focus, focus on using every moment as effectively as possible.

Mess = Busy Now   Clean = Complete

Let's talk about a messy desk. During the workday, my desk is a mess. Why? Because I have at least three projects going at once, and that means notes, papers and materials, and my computer and phone going strong. A messy desk while you are cranking out great work is just fine.

The mess is a sign that you have a lot going on and you're really focused on your work. And what about people who sit through the entire day with a perfectly neat desk? They might be incredibly tidy, but often they're really bored.

However, leaving the chaos to build up day after day on your desk is not a great idea. At my very first job in public accounting, my boss had a rule: Every day when you left, your desk had to be clean. This simple lesson has been a major tool in helping me in my career. It wasn't easy for me, but I had to do it, and it soon became a habit. It's a great method to help you finish what you have to do that day and make a clean break. That clears your mind so when you go home, you can focus on the other things you need to accomplish. More importantly, when you walk into work the next morning, you will have a better attitude and be more productive. The mess is necessary when I'm in the middle of all-out work and juggling tasks. But when I'm done, I straighten every-thing up, cross those finished tasks off the list, and start the next day with order instead of chaos.

So try this method starting today. Whatever time you leave your job, start winding up ten minutes earlier. Make this a habit! Make notes about what you have finished that day and what needs to be done tomorrow. Then put everything neatly away. Yes, sometimes I still have piles on my desk, but they are neat and organized for tomor-row. Everything is filed where it should be. Try this tactic for two weeks and it will become a habit because you'll love the way you feel when you walk into the office the next day.

Each morning, you are at an advantage when you start with an organized workspace. Unfinished or new tasks will be much easier to tackle, and you'll do them more efficiently. You'll notice your mood improves, your frustration level lowers, and you will feel ready to focus on your first challenge of the day. You know where everything is, so you can get right to work on the important things on your to-do list.

Keep the Whole Picture Focused

Let's look at focus in another way. When I owned a bookstore chain, people constantly asked me why I didn't put small coffee shops in my stores like many of my competitors. Well, it was a great idea to have coffee in stores, because I do believe the cappuccinos and crumb cakes add to a store's sales. But I decided not to do that. Why?

I didn't include these items in our stores because I felt strongly that we, a small business, needed to focus on what we really knew how to do—sell books. Our core business was books, not beans. If we had branched into coffee, we would not have done as great a job at selling books. Recommending a certain pastry is one thing, but talking to a customer about what kind of novel she'd like to read on her vacation is another. In addition, we didn't have the budget to branch out into a whole new product line and teach our employees to care for coffee machines, plates and garbage when they would rather be talking to customers about books. The employees' diluted focus might have made each task—selling books, selling coffee—only half as good as each should be.

When you are distracted, you won't be as successful. Weight Watchers, the weight loss giant, sold off its magazine and packaged food businesses because its owners wanted to concentrate on the company's core business, its fee-based classes. In a recent *New York Times* interview, the president of a small medical diagnostics company discussed how, during the early stages of his business, he was unfocused, trying to run several different businesses at once. Only when he sharpened his focus, concentrated only on the diagnostics company, and attacked the important tasks needed to get the company's business moving did he find success, building a company that generates $12 million a year in sales.

I believe that when you start a business or career, you should focus your efforts. When I owned a children's clothing store, I decided I wanted to open a ladies' clothing store, too. It seems like a natural progression—they're both retail apparel stores, very similar businesses. But I found that they're quite different. The markets were obviously different. The logistics of running these two businesses were also challenging: I had to go to purchasing shows at different times, and the advertising and marketing for each store were very different. I **Focus your** couldn't focus properly on each business because **efforts** of those differences, so eventually I got out of the ladies' clothing store and focused solely on the children's store. Later, I sold the children's clothing store to focus on my new venture, a chain of retail bookstores. To run a retail store, not to mention more than one store, and to be the hands-on owner and manager takes total focus.

No matter what your vocation—or even if you are running a household and raising a family—total focus is
what you need to be successful.

Focus on the Most Important Matters

Focusing can be difficult, because there are many distractions in life. It's difficult to focus on your relationship
when your business is a mess, and vice versa. It's difficult
to focus on listening to your child's story about his day at
school when you're thinking about the bills, the groceries
you need to buy for dinner, and the repairs you need to
make on the car. But you can learn to focus for times
when it's really important to be tuned in.

Let's try an experiment. When you get to work tomorrow, pretend that your boss says if you get everything
done, you can leave at 3 p.m. Now, this
won't work for everyone. If you're a
receptionist and have to answer the
phones, you have to answer the phones
all day. If you are a waitress and wait
tables for a certain amount of time, well,
you just have to be there. But for many of you, this trick
will work. You'll be surprised that you will get everything
done by 3 p.m.—an amount of work that on most days
takes you until 5 or 6! Why does this happen? Because you
focus a lot harder when you have a goal that benefits you.
You'll spend less time chatting with co-workers about the
great new movie that just came out or emailing your
friends about last night's baseball game, or all the other
things you do during the day that distract you from work

**Think about
what you can do
rather than what
you cannot do**

(and we all do these things).

Many internal and external distractions can cause you to lose focus. Perhaps the weather is bad, or there is terrible traffic slowing your commute. Perhaps you have a cold or you are angry with a difficult co-worker. You can overcome these distractions. Try the following techniques:

1. **Check in with yourself mentally as you are working on a difficult task.** Step back from your work and think about where you are, where you need to go, and what the next step is. Center your thoughts on the task at hand, rather than the negative distractions that are slowing you down. If you're trying to complete a sales report but find yourself thinking about the lasagna you have to make for dinner, step back and say to yourself, "Hey, focus on this sales report, get it done and then you can clear your desk and make it home in time to start cooking."

2. **Try a little positive self-talk.** Cheer yourself on with thoughts like "Great job on that last sales call," or, "You can make it that last mile on the treadmill." Encourage yourself during discouraging times so you can remain focused on what you need to do.

3. **Remove negative phrases from your verbal and internal vocabulary.** Think about what you can do rather than what you cannot do. People who constantly use "can't," "won't," "don't" and "never" create their own obstacles to success. Speak positively and focus on what is possible. If you seek a promotion at

work, focus on what makes you great for the job, not on the skills or the experience you may lack.

4. **Visualize yourself achieving your goal.** Rather than daydreaming, visualization is pure focus on what you wish to accomplish. Visualize each step you will take along the way to your goal. If you wish to run a marathon, visualize yourself training, running one mile, then two, then five, and so on.

Focus, focus, focus applies to all areas of your life. Let's say you are single and want to find a new boyfriend or girlfriend. Well, then, make it your focus. Don't just say over and over, "I want someone in my life. If I only had a relationship, everything would be better." That's wishful thinking, or worse, whining. Focus on finding someone great and make it happen.

Do all the things we have talked about in the previous chapters and focus on them. Get out there and network. Call everyone you know. Don't take no for an answer when someone tells you this guy or that lady is not the person for you. Believe me, people find it easy to tell you why something won't work for you—sometimes out of jealousy— but only you can really decide that. If you want to accomplish something, do the right things to make it happen. If you're a single woman and you want to meet your future husband, don't sign up for a knitting class—sign up for a hiking outing or go sailing on the lake. Focus on what you need to do to get what you want.

Visualize each step you will take to your goal

Be realistic and focus on what you can accomplish today. Don't forget that everything is an opportunity to meet someone terrific, so wherever you are, keep your eyes open...in the hardware store, at the bank, in your neighborhood as you're walking the dog. Put a smile on your face so everyone sees your fantastic attitude and wants to get to know you better. When you exercise, focus on the moves you are doing. Feel your body working—don't just go through the motions. I have a friend who works out at the same gym I do. Although she works out often, she has not seen the same results that I enjoy. I asked my trainer why this was happening. He said that she is probably going through the motions during her workouts, trying to complete the moves without focusing on doing each move as effectively as possible. Concentrate and you will exercise more effectively.

Try to Focus on a Daily Basis

Organization, which we discussed earlier, goes hand in hand with focus. Organization helps you focus on the steps you must take to achieve your goals. Each night before I go to sleep, I take some time to focus on the next day and what I need to do. It is amazing how many times I come up with a more efficient, faster way to complete every task. I think about the things going on at the office and even what I will need to wear.

As I'm driving in my car, I also do this exercise. Sometimes planning ahead is easier in the car because you're already moving. For some people, trying to focus when they're lying down, ready to sleep, isn't as effective. If you have trouble falling asleep at night because you can't let go of the day's concerns, plotting out tomorrow may help you let go.

Getting a good night's rest as often as possible is essential. You will not be able to focus and work effectively if you are not well rested. Many studies have shown that sleep deprivation leads to less effective job performance and poor health. Don't cut back on your sleep—your attitude will improve dramatically when you are rested and energetic.

"Get the maximum result for the effort you put forth so you don't waste time and energy."

It's helpful to check in with your to-do list on a daily basis so you know you're on track. Things can easily slip your mind, and then you will feel frustrated and angry at yourself for forgetting to do something important, like picking up a get-well card for your sick aunt while you are at the supermarket buying groceries. Try setting deadlines for yourself for some tasks, and use the reward system we talked about in Chapter Two when you accomplish something.

A good night's rest helps you focus

Rewards certainly help me stay focused on what I need to do. Sometimes I do something as simple as putting a sticky note up in my car with all the errands I have to do that day. Little reminders help me focus.

Focus on what you really want. Focus on where you are going. Focus on the project at hand. Tap into your positive attitude and do it right. You'll be pleased with the results and be able to move on to what's next on your list, and that is one step closer to where you really want to be.

- Are you easily distracted by office politics, outside concerns or personal problems that keep you from focusing on the task at hand? What steps can you take now to help you stay focused?

- Do you worry constantly about what other people think about you or your actions? Are your fears realistic?

- Do you often make a "to-do" list or do you struggle to stay on top of your tasks? Would you be more organized if you had special tools to help you? Have you tried any computerized tools?

- Do you struggle to "let go" of the day's problems, taking them home with you? How can you draw a line at the end of the day, putting some problematic tasks off until you return to work the next day? What changes can you make now?

Passion and Enthusiasm

The secret of genius is to carry the
spirit of the child into old age, which
means never losing your enthusiasm

~ ALDOUS HUXLEY

WHEN A PERSON HAS PASSION AND ENTHUSIASM for life and work, it shines through in everything they do. Dorothy would never have made it to the end of the yellow brick road if she had not been so passionate about getting back to her family, and so enthusiastic about making it to see the wizard. She didn't let anything stand in her way. You always have a choice, and your choice should be, like Dorothy, to really go for what you want. Your choice should not be acceptance of a status quo that isn't really satisfying. Make the choice to pursue your passion and let your enthusiasm carry you home.

What are passion and enthusiasm? Why do these two components of a great attitude go hand in hand? Passion is an intense emotional drive or excitement.

Passion drives you to go after what you desire

It drives you to go after what you desire. Enthusiasm is intense, eager interest in something. To achieve the goals you pursue, and to overcome the inevitable obstacles and setbacks you may face, you must have passion and enthusiasm. Otherwise, you will stall.

Passion and enthusiasm also help create successful business and personal relationships. A good example is when you walk into a bookstore and ask an employee to recommend something for you to read. If that person says to you, "This book is good," you may not be convinced enough to buy it. But if they say, "You must read this book, because I read it and it is soooo great," you will probably buy it! Even if it's a book that you may not normally pick up, you might give it a try because that person pitched it to you with such passion and enthusiasm. That is the heart of a good salesperson—he is passionate and enthusiastic about his product and what it can offer the customer.

I always told my staff that a book is the easiest product in the world to sell. All you have to do is find out what type of books the customer likes to read and then use passion and enthusiasm to recommend something in that genre. Once you do that, voila, the book is sold.

Passion Is Attitude Spelled Differently

What does this have to do with attitude? Everything. Passion and enthusiasm are really attitude expressed differently. I am a very passionate and enthusiastic person about the things I do and the people who surround me. Why? Because I believe in them. If I didn't, I would not surround myself with these people, activities, pursuits and objects. Of course, I love my friends and I love my family. I even love my gym; I believe I could sell a membership to my gym to anyone. I love my favorite places to eat. I love the clothes that I buy and wear each day. I love my work. I love my house and almost everything in it. I wouldn't have these things in my life if I did not feel passionately about them. You have to learn to love the good things in your life—that's part of having a good attitude.

Learn to love the good things in your life

It's important to be passionate and enthusiastic about the main pursuits in your life, such as your career, marriage or family and friends. I recently read about a teacher who interviewed some of her students to find out which faculty members they liked most and why. The students revealed that they preferred teachers with a passion for teaching as a profession, or perhaps a passion for the subject he or she taught. The students felt that a teacher with this sort of passion communicated the lessons more effectively to the students.

If you can't be enthusiastic about the things around you and you can't seem to change them, then change your attitude. Try to look at your work or surroundings in a new way; you might find something you haven't recognized before. Perhaps an old friend has qualities you've overlooked that are really inspiring – such as an ability to listen well.

When I look back at my time working in public accounting, I remember how much I lacked passion and enthusiasm for my work. Because I didn't like the work and didn't feel enthusiastic about doing it, I wasn't very good at it. If I had stayed much longer, I think the company would have fired me at some point. So I moved into a new career that I was much more passionate about: retail entrepreneurship, sales and marketing.

Until I moved on to my new career, I didn't realize how much I had lacked enthusiasm for accounting. I had always focused on the things I did like about my job—I enjoyed working with my colleagues and the paychecks —but I didn't really enjoy the work. If you feel that you lack passion and enthusiasm for your job, it may be time for change.

Compose a list of the things you like about your current job or profession: friends, the commute, the pay, the actual work you do each day. Concentrate on the positive and see if you can change the negative. Little by little, you may be able to change your attitude about some aspects of your job that you don't enjoy. If not, it may be time for a new position or an entirely new career. You can do it—I did.

Make the Most of What You Do Now

While I am doing something, I try hard to make the most of it. I look for the parts of things that do make me happy, and I try to focus on those aspects. I understand that this approach is not always easy when you've decided to move on to other challenges. I wanted to sell my bookstores for about two years before I found a buyer that fit. How did I keep my good attitude when I knew I wanted to move on? I focused on my original passion and enthusiasm for owning my business and for our customers.

I wanted to sell my business because I was ready to try something new. I always say, "Leave the party while you're still having fun." I was still having fun, but I knew in my heart it was time to move on to a new challenge. I'm truly an entrepreneur; I like the starting and building of a new business and establishing the brand in the marketplace, which involves public relations and marketing as well as management skills.

Once the creation of the business is complete, it is really time for someone else to take it to the next level. I was ready to hand it off to that person—but it took two years to find the right buyer. I spent those two years doing something I wasn't totally committed to. So in order to maintain my enthusiasm, I focused (see Chapter Seven) on the aspects of the business that I enjoyed, and I delegated other, less enjoyable parts of the work when possible. I loved marketing, so I spent a lot of time making our marketing the best it could be. I focused on branding our name so it became a household word in the book industry. I learned a very valuable lesson during this time: You will be happiest, most enthusiastic and most passionate if you are doing the things you love. And when doing something you are easily passionate about, usually you will be more successful, whether you are a stay-at-home mom or a computer technician or a physical therapist.

Do the things you love to do

I recently read a newspaper article that said American workers can be divided into two camps: those who love their work and those who do not. If you struggle to find passion and enthusiasm for what you are doing now, do not give up hope. Change is possible. You are not stuck in one profession for your whole life. Search for the occupation or lifestyle that will make you happy. Examine your hobbies or extracurricular activities to pinpoint your passions. Do you enjoy sailing and can't wait to leave your desk each week to head to the lake? If so, why not pursue a job that brings you closer to sailing, such as selling sailboats or sailing gear, or managing a marina? Do you enjoy being with animals? Why not start a pet sitting business or learn to groom dogs? Or manage a kennel or sell pet care products to veterinarians? It may not be feasible for you to make a dramatic career switch right away, but if your passion is taking you in a new professional direction, go with your enthusiasm. Find a way to pursue your passion so you feel enthusiastic about each day.

People who love what they do often don't view their

jobs as work, but rather as a passionate challenge or a pursuit of a goal. These are the people who get ahead. I recently read about a leading home builder who saw passion as a major component of his effective leadership. He described how he viewed his job as competing with himself to constantly do his best, and how could he not be passionate about that? Effective leaders are passionate and transmit that passion to the people who work for them. As the owner of my company, I had a passion for the business. I came to work each day believing that we were creating the best bookstores in the city, stores that would offer our customers the best selection of books at the best prices, with knowledgeable employees who would help customers choose the right books.

On its official web site, the technology company United Experts describes its employees as people who "love and enjoy what they are doing...Our enthusiasm is exactly what distinguishes our company from our competitors, and it is contagious." Passion and enthusiasm are contagious. When you are around people who express passion and enthusiasm for their **Passion and** work or lives, you feel energized as well. If you **enthusiasm** surround yourself with people who speak neg- **are contagious** atively about their jobs all the time, or who complain constantly about their unsatisfying relationships and boredom, then chances are good that you will be bored and unhappy too. So surround yourself with people who have the same passion and enthusiasm for life as you do. That is what I do—my friends share my zeal for life.

Obviously, if you are in a relationship or a friendship that you are not enthusiastic or passionate about, it will suffer. You don't want to be close to someone if you are not passionate about them, and you don't want to spend time with people if you are not enthusiastic about doing so. If a relationship with a friend or significant other deteriorates badly, your lack of passion and enthusiasm will be obvious. Sometimes you can spark it again. In some cases, you may have to move on.

Remember: Nobody is perfect. A psychologist once told me that if you can get 50 to 60 percent of what you need from a friend or spouse, you're doing great. You need to get the rest of what you need from other sources: other friends, family, job, hobbies, or even yourself.

Start by Changing What You Can

You may be thinking, "I really dislike everything about what I am doing now, but I can't change right now. What can I do?"

It's not easy to suddenly change things, even if you are unhappy about them. First, think about what made you do this thing in the first place. Focus on that idea. This is where attitude is very important. You have to train yourself to use your energy to find the bright spots, because it takes the same amount of energy to deal with the bright as it does the dark. This takes practice and training. You must focus on finding the parts of your experience or relationship that make you smile. Use your skills to "make it happen" (see chapter two), and spend your energy on making it happen, rather than dwelling on how miserable you feel. Only you can create change. You can't expect things to change magically. If you're unhappy in your current job, start looking for a new one. It may take months or a year. But if you start today, you are already one step closer to your eventual goal. Be willing to put passion and enthusiasm into your search so you can make it to the end of the long road. If you are passionate about what you are doing, other people will sense it and know that you are serious about the opportunities you encounter. Research shows that passion and enthusiasm are more important than talent or aptitude in many cases. Interviewers will be impressed by your attitude and will be more willing to take a chance on hiring you instead of someone who has great experience but a glum attitude.

Research shows that passion and enthusiasm are more important than talent or aptitude

Passion and enthusiasm are equally important in your everyday life at home. This attitude can help you be successful in even the most mundane chores. Let's say you want the kids to go to bed, but they resist and want to stay up late watching TV. If you approach this challenge with a passionate, enthusiastic attitude, you'll be more successful than if you just scream and demand that they go to bed. You can tell them how much fun they can have in their rooms doing what they want for a while. They can read a book or play a game. I found that once I got my kids to go to their rooms, usually they went to bed soon afterward because they were tired. By not yelling or making demands, I created a more positive energy about bedtime and there was less friction between us. Everyone wound up happier!

How about getting your husband or wife to take out the garbage or help empty the dishwasher? A little passion in the asking will go a long way. Try something like, "Honey, it would mean so much to me and be such a big help if you could take the garbage out tonight." Make it sound as if the chore is something that would help you and make you happy, rather than taking a demanding approach that creates conflict and resentment. If you want help cooking in the kitchen, say, "Honey, I'm very lonely in the kitchen. Would you please come and keep me company?" Once someone is in the kitchen with you, watching you prepare the meal, it's hard for him or her not to help. I admit, it doesn't always work for me; sometimes my husband just comes in and sits down to talk. So I use my positive energy to focus on the fact that I'm happy I have someone to talk to. If I am really desperate for some help, I apply a little enthusiasm and ask for specific assistance. Like, "I'm rushing to make this beautiful meal for our family, so I would appreciate it if you would please set the table. It would help me out a lot."

We've all heard the horror stories of blind dates. Well, I had a few blind dates that I didn't like that much, but I always looked for the bright side of the people I met. Everyone has something interesting to offer, something you can take with you as you meet new people. I knew I didn't have to marry these dates, so I didn't worry about them not being perfect. I enjoyed learning about them and networking. You never know when someone will be helpful in your life. Take the approach that everyone is an opportunity. Enjoy meeting the person and don't dwell on the parts you don't like. You cannot be attracted to everyone. You can, however, be passionate and enthusiastic about the process and your eventual goal of finding happiness.

If you struggle to find something to be passionate about in your life, it's time to do a soul search. Sit and write some thoughts about the things you were passionate about in the past. Perhaps you used to play sports when you were in high school, but you eventually gave them up as an adult because of lack of time, family and job. You might miss the excitement of playing a sport, being outdoors and active, and competing with others. Do something about it! Rekindle the passion and enthusiasm you once had for what you loved. Look around your community for an adult softball league or start a bowling team at work. Ask your friends if they would like to go out and toss a base- **Do a soul search** ball around in the park, or ask one of your kids or grandkids to do that. Chances are that they would love to! You would be amazed how much doing something you love will put passion and enthusiasm back in your life.

Adding New People and Activities Spark Passion

When you find yourself in a rut and lack passion for your life, trying something totally new is the greatest boost.

Meet a new friend or take a class in something you know nothing about, like a new language, wine buying or investing. Adding new experiences and new knowledge can often open doors in your mind. They lead to new opportunities, and we already know that new opportunities are golden. Often a lack of passion and enthusiasm occurs when your life and job have become routine. Adding something new will shake things up for the better! You will see what changes to make, where you want to go next and what you have to do to get there. Your attitude and energy level will go up. You don't have to discard everyone and everything in your life to spice things up—just add new people and activities to the mix so your attitude stays fresh. Adding something new lends a spark to everything in your life.

Travel is one great way to rejuvenate your passion and enthusiasm for life. I'm lucky in that my husband and I and our friends all love to travel. I've seen a variety of new places, met interesting people and visited incredible sites. Traveling has been very stimulating for me and helps me regain passion for my daily routine when I come back. Everyone needs time to rest and recharge.

Travel doesn't have to mean a long, expensive vacation to some distant location. You can travel to new places in your own community—read the local newspaper or local magazines to find new museums, neighborhoods, parks, restaurants or free concerts. Seek out day trips you can take by car with your family, perhaps to an historic site or natural wonder like a mountain, lake or park. If you enjoy traveling to distant places but find it expensive and daunting to plan, seek help from travel agents or travel websites that do the work for you. Be as passionate about your leisure time as you are about your job—the payoff is huge!

Passion and Enthusiasm Lead to Goals Accomplished

With almost every goal I have achieved, I know that my passion and enthusiasm have made them happen. When I wanted to secure celebrity book signings for my stores, I poured my passion and enthusiasm into research, brainstorming and presenting my case to the New York publishers—and won in the end. When I wanted a business loan to start my children's clothing store, I shared my passion and enthusiasm for my idea with the loan officer— and got what I wanted. When I was a divorced, single mom and wanted to get married again, I put passion and enthusiasm into meeting new people and finding the right guy—and I did. Passion and enthusiasm for what you really want lead to goals accomplished.

Be passionate about your leisure time

At the same time, you can't be passionate and enthusiastic about something that someone else wants for you if you don't want it for yourself. Trying to please others is not always easy or productive. Let's say your mother wants you to be the president of the PTA because of the prestige and because she was president of the PTA. However, you don't really care to be the president of the PTA. You dislike the meetings and would rather sit back and let someone else lead in this particular area of your life. How much enthusiasm will you put into running for that position? Not much! And you won't be successful.

Don't waste your precious time and effort trying to achieve the goals that others have set for you—focus on your own dreams and realize them. While we all have to do things that we don't enjoy (jury duty, going to the doctor, making sympathy calls to a friend who has lost a relative, preparing our taxes), you can approach **Focus on** everything with a positive attitude and some enthu- **your own** siasm. Jury duty may be a time to meet a few new **dreams** people, learn something about our judicial system or to read a book. Going to the doctor may be an opportunity to talk to your doctor about important health issues and improve your well-being. Making a sympathy call to a friend is an occasion to be kind to someone who may in turn be kind to you someday. Preparing your taxes is an opportunity to take a close look at your finances and identify areas where you can save money.

Be passionate and enthusiastic about everything you do in life; you will find yourself focusing on the important, positive things and eliminating those that drag you down. You'll accomplish more and waste less time. You'll feel better about yourself and move closer to what you really want.

- What things, people or activities are you most passionate and enthusiastic about?

- How can you spend more time and energy on those things and less time and energy on what you find boring?

- What aspects of your job or profession do you have the most passion for? Are there other jobs or professions that might allow you to do more of these?

- What activities can you seek out that will spark passion and enthusiasm for life, but don't cost too much money or time that you don't have right now? Are you willing to try one of these a month?

Everything Is a Sales Job

Defeat is not the worst of failures.
Not to have tried is the true failure.

~ GEORGE E. WOODBERRY

YOU ARE PROBABLY THINKING, "WHAT DOES SELLING have to do with a great attitude? I thought this book was about how my attitude is going to take me wherever I want to go."

You're right, this book is about attitude. But selling is at the heart of everything we do in life, and effective selling is an integral part of a great attitude. It doesn't matter if you're trying to get a new job, improve your love life, make new friends or be the captain of the tennis team. You have to sell, sell, sell it—your idea, your plan, yourself—to everyone around you in order to get what you want. If you have a defeatist attitude and convince yourself that nobody will buy what you have to offer, you won't get anywhere. So learn how to be a confident seller and there is no limit to where you can go!

When Dorothy made it all the way down the yellow brick road and finally came to the massive doors of the Emerald City, what happened? She knocked and asked to see the wizard, but the gatekeeper told her to **Selling is at the** go away and come back another day. Did **heart of every-** Dorothy give up? No—she sold her case to the **thing we do** gatekeeper and convinced him to open the doors. When the wizard dismissed her, did she just give up and accept that she would never get home to Kansas? No—she sold her cause to the wizard and won him over to her side. He even attempted to fly her home to Kansas himself in his hot-air balloon. Dorothy knew how to sell, sell, sell her spirited enthusiasm and get the assistance she needed to go where she wanted.

Think of Sales in a New Way

When most people think of selling, they picture the sales clerk in their favorite store. They envision a door-to-door vacuum cleaner salesperson, or even someone selling advertising for the local TV station. Selling is really much more than that—it's a key aspect to almost every job, but it also drives what we do in every part of our lives.

Think about everything you sell every day. Have you ever called the credit card company because they charged you a service fee for a late payment? You say that you weren't late, that the payment simply took too long to get to the company in the mail. You bargain with the customer service rep to get him to remove or reduce the finance charge. That's sales. You're selling your side of the story and selling your vision of the outcome that you desire.

Sell with spirited enthusiasm

Have you ever tried to convince your kid to put on a jacket on a chilly fall day? Your child doesn't want to wear a jacket, but you don't want her to catch a cold. So you plead, or you bargain, or you come up with a good argument for why this will benefit her more than please you. I call this "tactic selling". When you sell your point of view (wearing the jacket) with a good attitude, you'll be even more successful.

You have to believe in the value of what you are trying to sell in order to fuel your positive attitude. If you truly believe that your idea is great, you will sell it with passion and enthusiasm (as we learned in the previous chapter). The same goes for a product you are trying to sell, or even when you are trying to pitch yourself as the perfect person to fill a new job or get a raise or promotion.

Selling is important in dating and romance, too. That may surprise you, but it's true! If you're single, think about times when you've wanted to go on a date with someone you found attractive. You used sales to get that person to be interested in you. You sold your charm and attractiveness through flirting and compliments. Or you might have tried selling the date itself to the person you liked: a fun party, dinner at the new restaurant in town, two tickets to the hot new movie that just opened. More than anything else, when you like someone and want to spark a romance with him or her, you sell yourself with gusto. You promote your cause and put your energy and attitude into winning the affection of that person. That's a great sales job! There are some people who never seem to lack dates or romance, but who aren't the best-looking or the richest people. How do they do it? With charm, persuasion, passion and a great attitude. They sell themselves. They don't wait for people to knock on their doors—they go out and find great people and pursue them. If there is a free concert in the park, they don't sit home and say, "Gee, I wish I had someone to go with me to the concert. I guess I'll just stay home." They call people on the phone until they find someone who says yes, they'd love to go to a fun concert. They sell the concert so the potential dates line up!

If you're married or in a relationship, you use sales all

Believe in what you're selling

the time, but you may not realize you're doing it. Relationships are full of successful compromises. If you want to go to the movies but your husband wants to stay home and watch TV, you have to sell the idea of going to a movie to him. You might sell your plan by picking an action movie he'd love to see, or by offering to cook his favorite dinner if he'll take you out to a movie. It's the subtle art of persuasion, and if you do it with enthusiasm and skill, you'll win much of the time.

Put Together a Great Sales Pitch

In our jobs or companies, no matter what profession we are in, we sell all the time. We don't sell only products like carpeting or lawn mowers. We sell ideas and services, but on most days, we also sell change.

If you're reading this book, you probably seek some kind of change in your life. Most people do. But in order to implement change, you have to sell the change you seek to the people around you who can make it happen.

Let's say you want one of your coworkers to take your shift at work. You don't just ask them or tell them to do this; you must sell the idea. Any change at the office has to be sold to everyone. It **We sell all the time** can be a change in an idea or a procedure. Maybe you think that the company ought to offer a discount to frequent shoppers or do its record-keeping in a more efficient way. No matter what it is, if you truly believe that the change will make things better, then you can sell it to everyone else. Your passion in "selling" the change becomes your greatest asset.

Here is one example of selling an idea from my personal experience. When the second book in the incredibly popular *Harry Potter* series was about to debut, I knew that there would be huge interest in the book from both our customers and the media. I didn't want to just put the book on the shelves; I wanted the release of the new book in our stores to be a big event. I felt that a splashy event would excite the local press, and the ensuing media coverage would promote our stores over our rivals. I also believed that our customers would enjoy coming to a special event instead of just buying the book at some other time, and if they came to an event, they might buy more than one copy or even buy other things while they were there.

My idea was to create a slumber party. I wanted all the stores to be open at 12:01 a.m. on the day the books could officially go on sale. The kids in the neighborhood could come for games, cookies and storytelling, and then their mommies and daddies would buy the book as soon as it came out of the boxes. It was an exciting, innovative idea.

Well, my staff didn't really like my idea at first because they didn't want to work all night. I knew that it was going to be hard on them, so I had to sell the idea. I had to convince them that it would increase sales in their particular stores, which would lead to a bonus for them. I sold the idea that the slumber party event was unique and would get great media coverage—another boost for their store's sales and a potential bonus for them. (In a pinch, money always talks. If you can think of a sales pitch that translates to more money or more business for the person you are trying to sell, use it.)

I convinced them and we put on the slumber party event. It was a huge hit, both financially and in terms of media coverage for our store. The next day, the staff all thanked me for selling the idea so hard. They were won over by my sales pitch, because the pitch was offered with enthusiasm and a strong argument on how it would be a win-win opportunity for all of us.

Sell That Win-Win Angle

Many times when I have been interviewing someone for a job in one of my companies, I've found that I had to sell them on the benefits of working for us rather than choosing a job in a bigger business that had more financial benefits. That's not always easy, but it is worth doing. If you believe in the value of what your company has to offer beyond money, you can sell the job as a great opportunity. You have to appeal to the person's deeper desires and present the job as a win-win.

A valuable position at my book company was our director of public relations. I knew that we were not able to offer candidates as much salary as they might be able to earn at other PR jobs, so I convinced interviewees that our products almost promoted **Appeal to the** themselves. Every book tells a story, so if you're **person's** creative (and PR professionals thrive on **deeper desires** opportunities to be creative), it's fairly easy to get the media to cover what you are pitching. With this approach, I convinced the interviewee that he or she would get to be creative in a job that was exciting and fun. They could see the results of their work, and even see their name in the media as the spokesperson for the company. They would work in a casual environment that promoted entrepreneurship and creativity. These are all big selling points for someone seeking a position in this field. While the salary may not have been as high as they would find in other jobs, the winning selling point was the casual work environment and the creative, fun nature of the job. In the end, I always got a good response from people I interviewed.

Of course, in some situations, you will find that your sales pitch is not successful. How do you respond? First, remember what we discussed in Chapter three—never take "no" for an answer. Figure out another approach and see if you can convince the person to agree with your vision. If that doesn't work, consider moving on. There are some people you can't sell your idea, product or vision to—but there will be others who will be a better fit. Forcing a "fit" often doesn't work very well, as you probably already know. The nature of a win-win is that it works. It becomes clear to everyone involved that this is a win-win situation. Your win-win situation is out there, so spend some time and effort looking for that perfect fit.

Spend time looking for the perfect fit

Great sales techniques can help you approach any selling situation with ease and confidence. Here are a few techniques I swear by:

1. **Prospect.** Do research about customers (or donors, if you are fundraising for charity, or even

dates, if you are single and looking for a mate) who seem to have the most potential. Know as much as you can about the other person before you go in, and use this information to craft your approach. Plan a pitch that defines your idea as a win-win situation. Of course, we know that we don't take no for an answer. What we do is present another angle so we can try harder for that yes. Think of various reasons why the prospect might say no, and then come up with great rebuttals. That way, you won't hesitate and you'll appear confident, even if the person says no.

2. **Qualify.** When you begin your proposal, ask questions to determine their needs, their limitations (such as budget), and their goals. Through these questions, you will determine if this person is really a viable customer for what you are selling or the idea you are presenting.

3. **Pitch.** Present what you are selling to the customer. Give a firm handshake, look the person in the eye and smile! These three things sound old hat, but they are very important. If you are trying to sell something, greet the prospect with cheer and confidence. Smile and look them in the eyes so the meeting gets off to an upbeat, positive start. People enjoy being around positive energy. They are attracted to it. A weak handshake, wandering eyes and a weak smile send a signal that you lack confidence in yourself and your idea. So send the right signal—that you mean business.

Be prepared with any information you may need, such as financial data, background material or even visual aids like charts, design sketches or photographs. Preparation indicates that you are serious about what you are doing.

Belief in yourself is the most powerful tool you have

Describe how your product or idea will serve their needs and add value to what they are trying to do. Be positive about what you have to offer, rather than negative about what your competitors may offer. Talk up your idea, but don't disparage the ideas of others that differ from yours.

4. **Seal the deal.** Don't leave anything hanging. Sign the papers, make the date, agree on terms and set your next appointment to move forward.

Believe in It and You Will Sell It

Your belief in yourself, your idea or whatever you are selling is the most powerful tool you have to create a successful outcome. You can't sell anything well—particularly yourself—if you don't believe in it. A good sales job and a passionate argument often win the day. If you don't believe me, watch *Court TV* trials for a few days. Lawyers always make passionate arguments for their clients' positions, although we know that many times their clients are at fault. There are two sides to every story, and you must sell your side with passion.

Probably the biggest obstacle to effective sales is fear. People fear rejection, embarrassment and failure. I often feel insecure about new challenges, too. But I let my fear of failure motivate me to do what it takes to succeed. Fight fear by eliminating most of its causes.

Fear is caused by:
- Lack of skills or confidence in your abilities
- Lack of preparation
- Low self-image
- Desperate desire for approval
- Defeatist self-talk

Eliminate these causes one by one.
- Have confidence in the abilities you do have, and realize that everyone cannot be proficient in everything. Learn what you can in order to build your skill set, and seek the expert advice of people you know who have the skills you lack.
- Preparation is key. If you have a presentation to make, practice for a few days before the event. Take the time to do your research about a company or person. If necessary, schedule fewer sales calls so you can do your homework properly. Don't just walk in and wing it.
- Improve your appearance to boost your self-image. Wear your power suit or your favorite outfit to a sales call. Get rid of clothes that don't make you feel your best. Keep your hair, nails and face well groomed. People will perceive you as someone who has his or her act together, and you will feel more confident.
- The only approval you need is from yourself. Congratulate yourself for doing a good job, even if

you don't make the sale. It's not the end of the road. There are many more sales to make.

- Talk yourself up at all times. Don't say to yourself, "I'll try, but this guy will never say yes." Believe that he will say yes before you walk in the door, and tell yourself over and over again that he will say yes. Tell yourself that you are a confident, successful person who has just what the customer wants. You are in charge.

Anyone can sell anything to anybody if the salesperson's attitude is right. There is a guy in my hometown who sells vacuum cleaners for a living—and does it very well. That may not sound very interesting to you, but this man is passionate about his job. How does he approach selling something as common as a vacuum cleaner with such enthusiasm and success? He puts his mind and his heart into the pitch for his product. Selling is 100 percent attitude. You will sell successfully if you have a great attitude and transmit that attitude to the customers. Attitude stems from believing in what you want to happen and making it happen—and that's selling.

This guy thinks about the unique selling points of each vacuum cleaner and what features each one offers.

Selling is 100% attitude

He considers different types of customers and what features might appeal to each person. He starts off by getting to know his customer and learning their important characteristics: Do they have allergies? Do they have a dog that sheds a lot of hair? Do they hate to vacuum? Do they have a house with lots of stairs or an apartment that is all on one floor?

Once he knows more about his customer, he sells the right vacuum cleaner to suit his customer's needs and desires. Most people would simply choose one model and try to sell it to the customer with vigor. But this guy knows that most people are looking at the cheapest model, and he wants to sell higher-priced models, something known as "up-selling." So he starts with a lower-priced model and then gently begins to tout the added benefits of pricier, more powerful models. He uses psychology to convince his customer that the more expensive vacuum cleaner with more features will make vacuuming easier. The pricier model will suck up more dirt and allergens than the cheaper model. By getting to the heart of what the customer really wants and needs, he can sell a $800 vacuum cleaner to someone who walked into his store to buy a $250 model. It's all because he does his research, practices his approach and considers each customer's unique situation with care. And he doesn't take no for an answer!

Sell to suit your customer's desires

Remember, a "no" doesn't always mean that you are facing a dead end. In some cases, you may realize that your selling strategy isn't going to get you everything you want. But can you push harder and get some of what you want? Some is always better than none, and it may allow you to push closer to your ultimate goal. IBM recently did a study in which it found that peak sales performers pitched customers an average of five times, while average salespeople pitched customers only once—then gave up at the first no. Successful people keep trying.

Do car salesmen take no for answer? Rarely! They're known for not giving up, even though you say you are not interested in buying their car. Why not turn the tables and sell the deal you really want to them? If the deal isn't as attractive as you like, ask the salesperson to throw in free oil changes for a year, if he can't lower the price of the car anymore. If there is a company that you really want to work for but the employer isn't offering you the job you want, sell the idea of your working there part time or on an interim basis. Once he sees how competent you are on the job, he'll probably offer you a full-time position.

If you have a job that involves doing something you don't really believe in, it's time to take stock of your situation. Can you step back and figure out a

No doesn't always mean a dead end

pitch that you do believe in? Perhaps you sell air conditioning systems and find this boring. You say to yourself, "Who really cares about this stuff? It's the same thing every day. An air conditioner is an air conditioner. How can I get motivated to do my job?"

Take a minute to think about what you really do each day. You are playing a vital role helping homes and businesses operate more efficiently. You are making your customers' daily lives easier and more productive. The situation is a win-win for you, too, because you are developing relationships with people that will carry on as you move to new jobs in the future. If you are successful, they will recommend you to other customers and increase your company's business or your commissions.

If you can't get passionate and enthusiastic about helping people and making more money for yourself in the process, then you do need to find another job! Start networking (see Chapter Six) with friends, colleagues and contacts. You cannot be successful if you don't like what you are doing and can't find a way to be passionate about your product.

Get passionate about helping people

Volunteer Work Involves Selling, Too

Many of you have probably done some volunteer work at some point in your lives. It might be something informal, like pitching in to help the neighbor down the street mow her lawn. Or it might be something more formal, like getting involved in your local church, charity or political causes.

When you volunteer for an organization, you are also selling. Volunteers often fundraise for their organizations, asking businesses or friends for donations to the cause. A friend named Susan recently called to ask me to donate money to an annual fundraising campaign in our community. I knew that I wanted to give the same amount of money that I had given the year before, but she made a great sales pitch about how a little extra money, just $25 more, would have so many benefits for the cause. How could I resist? I raised my pledge by $25—all because of a great sales pitch. Fundraising is no different from sales. An effective fundraiser knows that the person can probably give $25 more, so he or she asks for it. An ineffective fundraiser might ask for too high an increase, such as $500, and wind up with no increase because the person gets angry. As in any kind of sales, a little research goes a long way. Knowing something about the person or company you are soliciting can help you make the right request—and get it.

Recently I volunteered to be the co-chairwoman of a big celebration for the anniversary of my favorite summer camp. Although the celebration would be a reunion for many former campers, we also hoped to encourage people to support the camp (a non-profit community camp) financially and to send their children there. I was passionate about supporting the camp, so I sold the reunion and the idea of helping the camp to the potential "customers"—former campers and other influential people in our community. I worked on ad campaigns, wrote letters and talked up our event. In the end, the sales job worked—we had a huge turnout and the camp received a lot of positive exposure to parents who might send their children there for many summers to come.

When you work with others on volunteer projects, you also have to sell your ideas to them. Let's say you are volunteering with your neighbors on a community canned food drive. The rest of the volunteers think that it would be easiest to just have donations collected in one big bin in a central location. But you really believe that more canned food will be collected if you have several, smaller collection bins stationed throughout the community, so donors will not have to travel as far and may be more likely to donate. More bins would require some extra work on the volunteers' part, however, because

everyone would have to collect the food in more than one location, but you believe that the goal of collecting more food would be achieved by following your idea.

Volunteer work is all about teamwork. Even if you are "in charge," you have to build consensus. Make your case with your fellow volunteers and sell it to them as a win-win. In this particular example, you could posit that collecting more food is the most important goal, and that more people are likely to donate food if the bins are closer to their homes and offices. You could assign volunteers who live close to the bins in their areas to be in charge of collecting those donations, so it's easy for them, too. In the end, if you are passionate about your idea and make a good case for it, others will come to your side and agree.

While volunteer work is a fantastic way to network and meet people, you have to decide what type of organization you want to work with, and what type of volunteer work you really want to perform. If you do not believe in the cause or the way the organization is being run, move on to something else. There are too many good causes out there to waste your leisure time and energy on something that isn't enjoyable or fulfilling. Don't view volunteer work as an obligation—it's a donation of your extra time and energy. Choose a cause you believe in, people you enjoy working with and work that makes you happy. If you have to sell yourself on the idea of doing volunteer work and you don't seem to be buying, there's a reason! But if you find something that really turns you on, you will be sold on the idea immediately.

In the end, your most important customer is yourself.

You have to be sold on what you are doing, whether that is a job, a relationship, a sport you play, a friendship, a decision you make or a cause you are working to promote. You have to believe in yourself and what you are doing.

Above all, if you are going to achieve and maintain a great attitude, and if you are going to use that attitude to make positive change in your life and accomplish your goals, you must have balance. Balance is the **Your most impor-** hardest thing for most people to achieve. **tant customer is** That's why the next chapter is so important. **yourself** Read on.

- Can you think of ways that your job involves selling? Who are the best "salespeople" at your workplace?

- In what ways could you improve your "selling" ability at work or emulate those successful salespeople?

- What situations outside work involve selling? Can you think of incidents in the past when a good sales job would have saved you money or aggravation?

- Do you do any volunteer work or extracurricular activities? If so, could better sales techniques help you make those efforts smoother or more enjoyable?

Balance Your Life

The important thing to realize is that it takes
a team and the team ought to get credit for
the wins and the losses. Successes have many
fathers, failures have none.

~ PHILLIP CALDWELL

DOROTHY MADE IT OUT OF OZ BECAUSE SHE WAS A great multitasker. She juggled a lot of perils and responsibilities at the same time: running from flying monkeys, taking care of her somewhat hapless traveling companions, defeating the Wicked Witch, and sweet-talking the Wizard. She had her hands full, but she always managed to do it with optimism and a great smile.

The two tools Dorothy used to keep everything in perspective—other than those sparkling red shoes—were attitude and balance. She was hopeful and focused, upbeat and strong. But she also knew there were certain moments when she had to stop and sing a song, do a little dance, or enjoy some pampering in the Emerald City. Life isn't all about the battle. Life is about winning the ultimate goal of happiness, and enjoying the journey along the way.

Balance Is the Greatest Challenge

Balance can be one of the most difficult things for people to achieve. Most of us feel overwhelmed by all the responsibilities in our lives: job, spouse, kids, house, car, money, health. We seldom feel that we have the time we need for each important task. I'll let you in on a secret: You will never have all the time you want or need to make every dream possible or to achieve perfection. But you do have time in each day to take care of the important matters in your life and still tend to your career. Too many people think that they have to put their loved ones or their personal needs on the back burner, leaving them to simmer while they focus on work and nothing else.

They hope that the relationships they ignore will stay intact until they can get back to them later on—but when does later on actually come? They hope that their health will take care of itself while they spend endless hours at the office and forgo regular exercise or healthy eating—but we all know this is a dangerous approach.

"You will never have all the time you want or need to make every dream possible or to achieve perfection."

Think of Dorothy's house in "The Wizard of Oz," flying around in the tornado. In a house that is out of balance, the furniture and people inside would tumble out of control. Your life is no different. Without balance in your life, your life tips too far in one direction, and everything tumbles over. Nothing can stand firm.

Do you tend to hone in on one thing and forget about everything else? People who do this **Don't put all** often wind up very sorry in the end. It's unwise to **your eggs in** focus only on your job and ignore your family or **one basket** friends. If you do, you'll soon lose your family and friends. It's much more rewarding to create a lifestyle that is balanced, where you can devote as much time as possible to many important things, instead of focusing on one thing and sacrificing the rest.

Zig Ziglar, the famous motivational speaker and business consultant, spoke recently about a study examining a cross-section of people in various professions, from blue-collar workers like truck drivers, to professionals like psychiatrists and CEOs. The people in this study who had created some kind of balanced life earned twice as much money as those in their fields who did not have balance, and the balanced group also felt happier, healthier and had more positive family relationships.

Let me tell you about a friend of mine, Gina, who is a dynamic, beautiful, young business executive. She started her own magazine publishing company and is a terrific success. She is driven and ambitious, and worked long hours building her business. But she felt that she could focus on only one thing at a time and be successful. With all her attention on her company, she believed she couldn't focus on meeting a guy and having a relationship. She just didn't think she could do it. So she stepped aside and let someone else run her company.

Concentrate on balancing each day of your life

Although Gina did what she felt was necessary to achieve her goal, I disagree with her and told her so. I feel that she shouldn't place all her focus on just one thing. I feel that she needs to create balance in her life and enjoy success in various areas. She needs to delegate certain tasks and have more support so she can run her business *and* have time to date. I believe that you shouldn't place all of your proverbial eggs in one basket. If you do, you run a high risk of dropping that basket and breaking all of your eggs. You must have balance in your life to keep your attitude in great shape.

All Priorities Can't Be No. 1

I firmly believe that achieving and maintaining balance

is a daily process. Don't think about balancing the next year or the rest of your life. That's too daunting. Think about balancing life one day at a time. Organization will help you immensely, and I provide some guidelines in this chapter for more effective organization. But you must also remember that your life is full of many important people, pursuits and passions, including your family, your friends, your job, your community, and yourself.

I urge you to spend part of every day doing what is important to you. Be in touch with the people in your life who are important. I use my cell phone to call people while I am driving to and from work. I talk to my friends and family members so I know what is going on with them and so they know I am thinking about them. I spend time talking to my children and time with my husband. I tend to these relationships and give them the nourishment they need to thrive. By planning each day carefully, I find time to spend talking to my loved ones and friends and also have plenty of time to do my work. Because I know that I have taken care of my personal relationships, when I am at work, I can focus on the job at hand. I am not distracted.

Spend part of every day doing what is really important to you

Having balance means that no one priority is so important that it thrives at the expense of everything else in your life. Of course your job is important. Of course your family is important. Of course your church is important. But remember: You are important, too. Without balance, you won't be healthy or happy, and you won't be able to enjoy the many things that life has to offer. With balance, you can enjoy a full life and achieve many goals without burning out.

Where is your weakness? Most people in our society spend too much time at work, robbing themselves of the satisfaction that comes with a full and happy home life. Could you come home early one day a week, or go to work a little later one day each week? Could you plan one day that is just for your family, a day when you don't do any work? If your job does not allow any time for your family, it may be time to look for another job.

It's better to make a little less money and have more satisfaction from the other things in your life. Is it worth it to have lots of money in the bank if your marriage and family falls apart and your body fails because you never had time to exercise or rest? The answer is no. Balance and organization—planning what you must do each day to cover all of your obligations in equal measure – will allow you to be the "person who has it all." Having it all does not mean having all the money or glory. Having it all means having a balanced, satisfying life.

As a working mother, I often had to juggle professional commitments with obligations to my children, but I always made it a priority to be there for my children when they needed me. You may feel that your boss won't understand if you have to leave work for a parent-teacher conference at your child's school, or for a big soccer game. Some bosses may not understand and may not accommodate you, but other employers understand that family is important. Talk to your boss and figure out a way you can do your work and still fulfill your obliga-tions as a parent. You can do both, and more and more employers are embracing this idea and realizing that bal-anced employees are more productive employees.

Balance Your Life Day by Day

To achieve balance, you must plan each day carefully. I cannot stress this enough. Make a list of your priorities and recognize that each one is important in its own way. Take your list and your calendar or date book and sit down on the Sunday night before you begin your new week. Concentrate on your list of important tasks and goals and plan when you can reasonably accomplish as many of them as possible around your work hours. Can you call your best friend, who just started a new job and is a little nervous about it, on the way to work Monday morning? Can you pack your gym bag on Tuesday night so you have it on Wednesday evening when you leave the office and can head straight for the gym? Can you plan potential meals for your family's dinner each weeknight so you can go to the market one time and have the ingredients neces-sary to create nutritious, tasty meals? Having one planning night allows you to shut out the distractions and concen-trate on what you really need to do. Check your list as you go through the week and cross off accomplished tasks. As you do this, you will feel an incredible sense of satisfaction, because you are getting things done! And you are touching the people who are most important to you.

Don't try to cram a million things onto your list, or you will wind up feeling like you have failed. Balance is achieved gradually by concentrating on doing the best you can day by day. Writer Sally Helgesen says that women who focus more on balancing their individual days rather than their lives are best at achieving balance. Instead of using a "tunnel vision" approach and devoting huge blocks of time to one project just to get it done, balanced people focus on creating a satisfying, complete day. If you try to achieve balance each day, then all the days will fall into place and form a balanced life.

Balanced life= a good attitude Nothing has to suffer, because everything receives enough nourishment and attention. A person who has a balanced life will have a good attitude. It's that simple.

Your health is most important. You won't have the fuel to live a balanced, busy life if you let your health slide. (In Chapter Eleven, I'll give you some of my favorite tips for staying fit and healthy.) Your family is very important. If you turn your back on your spouse, parents or children when they are in a crisis because you "really have to be at work and can't deal with it now," you will regret it deeply. As the old saying goes, "No one on a death bed ever said, 'I wish I had spent more time at the office.'"

Build a Successful Team

To achieve balance, you must realize that you cannot control everything, do every task or micromanage every project. If you do, your attitude will suffer. A balanced person—a happy person—understands that one must create and utilize a great team to be successful.

Creating a team doesn't mean that you find other people to do everything for you while you manage the system from above. There are instances where you can delegate tasks to others. For example, when I started the bookstore business, I had one store to focus on, and that meant I could control many aspects of the day-to-day business. As we expanded to 13 stores, I had to **Trust in people** shift my focus to the bigger picture—overall marketing strategies rather than small marketing efforts in a single location—and delegate some control to others. I learned to let go and find qualified people to take over particular areas of my business. If you have trust in the people on your team, you can achieve balance.

You can also delegate to your team at home. Your home team is your family—not only the people you live with, but also your extended family, like parents, brothers, sisters, cousins and in-laws, as well as close friends or neighbors. My friends are also vital members of my team. As a working mother, I often had to rely on my close friends to help me out when I had a work emergency and couldn't leave to pick up my kids or some other important task. I could trust them and I was always willing to reciprocate when they needed help. Cultivate close friends—especially if you don't have family living nearby—so you can have people to rely on to help you in a pinch, and be ready to help them in return.

Even your hairdresser, your doctor, your bank teller or your refrigerator repairman may be members of your team, there to support you when you need them. They perform vital tasks that help you complete your goals. Depending on your situation, you may be the coach of this team, but no matter what, everyone has to take part in the action for the team to thrive.

Find great players

In my family, everyone is busy and each person has an important role to play. It's always been that way, even when my children were younger. Once they reached an appropriate age, they helped me by cooking meals, and as a result they gained independence and strength because they didn't rely on me to do everything for them. The same is true of spouses.

To have a successful team, you need to find great players for each important task. Your role is to gently manage the team and be a good team player yourself. Even if you feel you have all the responsibility at work and nobody to support you, you actually do have a team. Think of the people who work in accounting and handle the bookkeeping and pay the company's bills. Think of the administrative assistants who answer the phones. Think of the janitors who clean the bathrooms and empty the trash. Think of the person who repairs the jammed photocopier. All of these people are members of your team, and you rely on them to succeed at your job, whether you are the CEO or a secretary. If you own your business, you have a team as well: your banker, your postal worker, your landlord, your software salesman. Thank these people, because when you really need them, they will be there for you.

How do you recruit a great team? Networking (see Chapter Six) will identify important players, even if you don't use their services all the time. Keep a file of qualified people you can rely on, and contact them when you need their services, a favor or a referral. Refer them to other people who may be able to utilize them. With these teammates, you can share great ideas that make everyone more effective. Be willing to hand off a hot lead if you think it can benefit them (and won't sabotage your own goals). In return, you may learn that one regular customer is a nightmare, while another is a gem. You know you can depend on these positive team players in a pinch—they're people you can trust. That's great team playing!

Other coworkers—the negative team players—may be obstacles. They want to hog the ball all the time and care only about their own statistics. They stand in the way of the team's success because they refuse to work with others. These people usually keep the details of the projects private and won't let anyone else handle any details. They make your job more difficult, because of their bad attitudes, but their sourness doesn't have **Work with the** anything to do with you. They may be bitter **positive players** about their job situation or angry about their personal lives. They complain constantly about "problem" customers or bad sales, blaming everyone else for problems and never taking responsibility for their own misery. It doesn't matter. You have to work with these people, but you also have to stay positive so they don't drain you and make your job impossible. Don't let the negative players ruin your positive attitude.

Focus on the positive team players and work with them. Negative team players usually don't last long. Their poor attitudes are obvious to everyone, including the boss. They can't succeed if they don't work with other members of the team. If they play a vital part in your role

Six Strategies for Successful Balance

It is easy to tell you that you should balance your life, but how do you really do it? Here are my six strategies for successful balance:

1. List your top five priorities. Think carefully about the five things that are most important to you and list them. This list should remind you what needs the most attention. The five things don't have to be listed in any particular order, as some may be equally important to you. For me, the top five are work, family, friends, community activism and exercise.

2. Fit your top five into your calendar each week. Sit down with your list and your calendar and plan carefully how you will touch all five priorities in the week to come. For example, plan on calling your friends while in the car to and from work, plan to get up earlier on some mornings to make a workout class at the gym, plan a night spent with just your husband having a quiet dinner.

3. Try getting up 30 minutes earlier to exercise in the morning. This gets your exercise needs taken care of before you start your day. You will feel energized for the day and won't miss the extra half hour of lying in bed, believe me!

4. Do something nice each day for at least one member of your team. Each day, touch one of the important people in your life and

at work, make sure they do not disrupt your balance. Be as professional and positive as possible. Hopefully your good attitude will reduce the friction.

To have balance in your life, you must be a good team player and depend on others you can trust. If everyone works alone, then work stops whenever one person goes on vacation or has to be at home with his or her family. Work can continue in your absence if you are willing to share knowledge and tasks with those you trust.

A Winning Combination

I have been able to achieve balance over the years because I made myself focus on many different—and wonderful—aspects of life. I have made family and let them know you appreciate them. It can be something simple, like a verbal compliment or some encouraging words to a friend, or maybe bringing a bagel or a piece of fresh fruit to someone you rely on at work. Let people know that you do not take their friendship or teamwork for granted, and show them that they are important to you.

5. Focus on your time goals. I talked about the importance of focus earlier in the book, but if you are going to achieve balance, you need to focus on your schedule and get the important things done. Concentrate on how long it will take you to do what you have to do, and consider additional time like travel in the car or unexpected delays. Refer often to your to-do list and your list of priorities so you don't overlook something vital.

6. One day each week, be totally unprogrammed. Although you have a lot to accomplish, you also need rest to have enough energy to keep your attitude going strong. You can't plan every moment of your life. Take at least one day (for me, it's a weekend day) where you don't have a schedule. Be spontaneous and do something new, or just do nothing at all. Enjoy life and the people around you. On this day, clear your mind of to-do lists. Focus on what's meaningful to you.

career priorities, but I've also made community involvement a priority in my life. Volunteering in my community has enriched my life, and it also helped me build my business and led to many new friends.

Religion or spirituality helps many people to achieve balance. Studies show that people who regularly attend a worship service of **Volunteering can enrich your life** some kind earn more money, have fewer problems with drugs, have a lower divorce rate and have happier intimate relationships. I would be willing to bet that they also have better attitudes.

Here are some strategies I have used successfully in my pursuit of a balanced life:

- Write what you have to do so you can keep track of your schedule.
- Prioritize your tasks and make sure you concentrate on the most important things.
- Make a list of your goals on a daily, weekly and monthly basis so you don't lose sight of anything important.
- Set boundaries for various activities, including a set number of hours you work on average, and a set amount of time you spend interacting with your family. I spend at least 45 minute to an hour each day working on important things outside my job, whether it's a volunteer activity or some personal interest.
- Set aside a block of time for just you. Do something you love doing by yourself, whether it is a hot bath, a run by the river, a trip to the farmer's market or an hour with a good book. This time is sacred.
- Set aside times when other obligations cannot interfere with the scheduled activity. If Wednesday night is the night you spend cooking dinner with your family, then don't plan to attend a sales seminar on Wednesday night.

Health and fitness are priorities in my life, and achieving important fitness goals (like running a marathon or competing in duathlons in my late 40s, when in my late 20s I might have collapsed after running three miles) gives me energy that I never dreamed possible. Sticking to my credo of always having more than one iron in the fire keeps me balanced. I am not focused on only one business or career opportunity, but many at once. I find new challenges that satisfy my needs and fit into my busy schedule, and I remain flexible so I can do the things that are really important.

I believe strongly that achieving balance comes easiest when you are at your best physically and mentally. That's hard for many of us to achieve—I know! Ten years ago, I was getting a divorce and preparing to re-enter the dating scene. I had two children and a stressful, time-consuming career. At this tense time, I chose to start running. Why? It was a healthy outlet for my stress (rather than overeating or spending countless hours in front of the TV) and built my self-confidence. Within a year, I went from running two or three miles to competing in half-marathons, and I never looked back. I lost weight, gained muscle and developed a fit body. I found untapped reserves of energy and confidence within myself.

Balance comes easiest when you're at your best

To achieve physical balance, you must make the following three things priorities in your life: sleep, diet and exercise. Get enough—at least seven hours—of sleep each night. If you have trouble sleeping on a regular basis, see your doctor and discuss various remedies. Sleep gives you energy for the following day. People who do not get enough REM sleep, or deep sleep, each night feel tired and sluggish the next day, and are more prone to physical illness. If you have somewhere to go in the evening and you're too tired, consider a short power nap. Winston Churchill, Thomas Edison and Leonardo da

Vinci were all reported to be nappers. Eat a healthy diet and get regular exercise—two things I'll talk about in full in Chapter Eleven. Treat your body well, for you will need

> ## "It's important to list all of your priorities and recognize that each one is important in its own way."

it to carry you wherever you go throughout your life.

While I still love to eat chocolate and curl up with a good book, I don't feel as good about myself—physically or mentally—if I don't get exercise and eat correctly. Being in shape keeps me in balance and gives me the fuel I need to lead a busy, balanced life. That's why our last chapter focuses on your body—because you will never achieve a great attitude if you don't start with a healthy lifestyle.

- Do you think you live a balanced life? If not, what areas of your life require too much time or energy?
- If you spend too much time working or thinking about work, how does this imbalance negatively affect your life?
- Can you think of ways to adjust your schedule so you can spend more time focusing on family or yourself?
- What things would you rather spend time doing other than your job? What obstacles stand in your way?

Diet and Exercise

Ability is what you're capable of doing,
motivation determines what you do,
attitude determines how well you do it.

~ LOU HOLTZ

HAVE YOU EVER LOST THREE POUNDS? HOW DID IT make you feel? Did your attitude change? I'm betting that the answer is yes, and that is why this book includes a chapter on diet and exercise.

Having a healthy, fit body is absolutely essential to having a balanced life and a great attitude. Your body is the vehicle you use to get where you are going in life—only you can't trade it in on a new model like you can trade a car. You have to do the maintenance necessary to keep it running well, or you'll break down and won't be able to go anywhere. You have to keep the engine tuned and use only the best fuel.

Dorothy had a great attitude when it came to diet and exercise. She didn't just stroll down the yellow brick road to get to the Emerald City—she danced and skipped all the way. When she needed a quick snack on the road, she stopped for a healthy, crisp apple. By staying active and eating the right foods, you'll have the energy you need to accomplish your goals. You'll have a much better attitude if your body isn't holding you back!

In the previous chapter, we talked about creating and maintaining balance in your life. Many people struggle to feel as if they are in control of their lives, so you may have felt this way occasionally. If you're typical, the first thing you may do when you feel out of control is eat poorly and avoid exercise. But that's the worst thing you can do. Two things you really can control are what you put in your mouth and how you move your body. Controlling those two important actions will make a huge difference in how you feel and look. Once you have your body in control, your attitude will improve and you will be able to start tackling other important goals. My cures for every ailment are proper exercise, a good diet and sleep. You'll find that your overall health and well-being will improve dramatically if you make those three things a priority.

Feeling Your Best Boosts Your Attitude

Looking and feeling your best is important because when you feel good about yourself, your attitude soars and you can perform all the things we've discussed in this book at a higher level. I'm not talking about drastic lifestyle changes or unrealistic expectations. I'm talking about small, gradual changes that add up over months or years to make a big difference.

My cures for every ailment are proper exercise, a good diet and sleep

If you want to achieve the attitude that will take you where you want to go, you must start from the inside and work your way out. You can't change the things around you if you are unhealthy inside. Health and fitness should be a lifelong goal. Diet is a way of life, not a two- or three-month fad. It has taken me ten years to achieve my goals—I started slowly and worked through setbacks to build and maintain good, healthy habits in eating and exercise. After a decade of exercising regularly and getting guidance from a trainer, I've discovered new techniques that have taken me to the next level of fitness—a level I never dreamed I would reach! I never aspired to it—it just happened because I did it one day at a time.

Make Positive Changes and Stick With Them

Most people can lose weight by making drastic diet changes (grapefruits, canned shakes, cabbage soup), but later they gain back all the weight lost because they didn't learn a lasting way to eat for health. Think of the food you eat as the high-octane fuel for a car that has to last you a lifetime. Making smart choices when you can will lower your overall calorie intake and lead to weight loss. It may take time, but you will see the results, I promise.

If you know that your diet is currently unhealthy and that your weight is too high, it's time to make a change. You must make it happen. You must make shopping for and preparing healthy foods a priority. Choosing healthier foods at the store is easy. Just take the time to think about what you are buying, or make a healthy shopping list and stick to it.

You also must make regular exercise a priority. Consider these things essentials in your life and make time for them in your schedule. Don't skip your exercise appointment any more than you would skip an important business meeting.

I won't offer you a whole diet and exercise book in this one chapter. There are plenty of great books out there that focus only on this subject. But I will offer you my personal tips for maintaining physical conditioning and a high energy level that many people my age (and younger!) might envy. I haven't always been thin and fit, and I haven't always been able to wear the clothes I

Your attitude soars when you feel good about yourself

love to wear now. I changed my habits and my body through dedication and hard work. For most of us, there is no other way. You can do it, too. I believe anyone can, as long as he or she is committed to making positive changes and sticking with it!

Make healthy foods and regular exercise a priority

Tips for Eating Right

I endorse a well-rounded diet. Trying to eliminate whole groups of foods from your diet or to binge on one low-calorie food all the time is unhealthy. It just won't last, and you'll wind up gorging yourself on high-fat treats because you feel deprived. And then you'll feel discouraged. Why do this to yourself? I also believe that you have to do what works for you. I have a friend who is incredibly strict about every type of food that goes into her mouth. She looks great, but I couldn't restrict myself that much. Few people can.

If you eat a well-rounded but healthy diet, and make the right choices whenever you can, you will slowly achieve the weight level that is right for you. I am convinced that in the end, only calories matter—not carbohydrates, protein grams or fat grams. If you stick to a controlled calorie diet (your doctor or a nutritionist can determine the right level for you), the other things will stay in control, and so will your weight! I recommend writing down what you eat, including approximate calorie counts, so you can keep track of your food intake and make adjustments when necessary. This trick helps you stay honest. I try to keep my daily calorie intake under 1,500 (although if I am exercising at a high level, I let myself have a little more), and writing down what I have eaten lets me know what I have left for the rest of the day.

To understand what foods are better than others, read nutrition labels, consult the Internet (www.calorieking.com and www.nutri-facts.com are two useful sites), or purchase a cheap, paperback calorie counter at your local bookstore. You may learn that some treats you enjoy are far less caloric than others, and you can make healthy choices. *Picture Perfect Weight Loss* by Howard Shapiro, MD, (Prevention Health Books) has been very helpful to me. This book shows **Quality foods** through clear visual images that you can eat **over high-** much larger portions (sometimes two or three **calorie treats** times as much) of healthy, low-fat foods than unhealthy foods for the same number of calories. I prefer quantities of quality foods over small amounts of higher-calorie treats. When checking nutritional information, don't forget to take note of serving sizes. If the label states that the whole box is one serving, then you know how much you are eating. But if it says 2.4 servings are in the box, you might want to measure your serving to be sure you're not overeating.

I prefer to eat small meals and snacks throughout the day, rather than one or two big meals and nothing in between. Research shows that eating smaller meals more often speeds up your metabolism, leading to better weight control. I never leave the house without several pieces of fresh fruit or an energy bar (but don't eat these like candy!) to satisfy my hunger between meals. It's better to keep healthy snacks on hand than to run to the vending machine at work for chips or chocolate bars. Your well-rounded diet **Healthy snacks** should include snacks in moderation, **throughout the day** because those snacks will make you feel less deprived. Some of my favorite snacks are graham crackers with peanut butter, toasted bagels with the doughy insides scooped out (they're crispier and lower in calories) spread with a little peanut butter, fresh fruit, frozen yogurt and energy bars. Never let yourself get hungry. As soon as you feel hunger coming on, grab one of those healthy snacks so you don't binge later on.

Eating Out and Eating on the Go

One thing I do before eating out is to have a healthy snack to curb my appetite. If you normally have a morning staff meeting where doughnuts are served, eat a satisfying, healthy breakfast at home first, so you will be less inclined to eat the high-fat goodies at the meeting. Or, you could have something small but satisfying at home to keep you from feeling hungry, then bring a healthy, delicious snack to the meeting. Eat a low-fat muffin, a small bagel or a piece of fresh fruit, while others are stuffing glazed doughnuts into their mouths. Or, you can keep your healthy snack at your desk so you know it's there when you get back from the meeting. It's easier to skip the doughnut if you know your delicious snack is waiting for you.

I actually have little will power. If I love a certain food,

I usually can't resist and cannot stop eating it. So I make every effort to keep it out of my sight. On occasion I have resorted to desperate tactics, but who cares? They work! If I'm at a restaurant or a dinner party and feel myself slipping, I will take pepper or salt or a sauce that I don't like and quietly pour it all over my favorite food so I won't eat it. I'm not kidding. And it works. If someone leaves irresistible leftovers in my house, and nobody else is eating it, I throw it down the disposal. It's gone.

Skip the doughnut, go for a healthy, delicious snack

When I first married my husband Richard, we had a party and there was a rich dessert left over. Richard came home the next evening and said he had been thinking about that cake all day. He couldn't wait to have a piece! I had to inform him that there wasn't any cake left, because I had put it down the disposal. He was shocked,

"Never let yourself get hungry."

but I told him that if I hadn't thrown the cake out, there wouldn't have been any left for him anyway. I would have eaten it all myself. Do what you have to do to succeed.

Parties and social occasions can be tempting. Obviously your host will prepare lots of delicious goodies to serve, but you must exercise restraint so you enjoy the occasion without wrecking your whole diet. First of all, have a healthy snack before leaving home so you aren't ravenous when you walk in and face a tray of cheese puffs or brownies. If possible, avoid the room where the food is

Party Do's & Don't's

Do...

Nibble on lowfat crudite's like baby carrots dipped in salsa (8 calories).

Enjoy healthful finger foods like grapes (10 grapes, 16 calories)

Choose healthy appetizers like $1/2$ ounce smoked salmon on a multigrain cracker (35 calories).

Fill up on raw vegetables (1 cup of mushrooms, zucchini or red peppers has 25 calories).

Head for the turkey-carving station (3.5 ounces has 136 calories).

Scoop up some wild rice ($1/2$ cup has 83 calories).

Have a whole wheat roll without butter (69 calories).

Savor refreshing sorbet ($1/2$ cup has 100 calories).

Enjoy a plate of fresh fruit (2 cups has 100 calories).

Munch on Almonds (1 cup has 70 calories).

Unwind with a cup of hot herbal tea, a relaxing nightcap (no calories).

Don't...

Snack on fattening chips and dip (about 175 calories).

Load up on greasy finger foods like buffalo wings (160 calories).

Top a Town House cracker with a chunk of Cheddar Cheese (1 cracker 18 calories; 1 ounce cheddar, 100 calories).

Get creamed on creamed spinach ($1/2$ cup has 169 calories).

Head for the prime rib-carving station (3 ounces has 300 calories).

Get stuffed on mashed potatoes ($1/2$ cup has 179 calories).

Wolf down two mini croissants (130 calories).

Go for ice cream ($1/2$ cup has 250 calories).

Indulge in a slice of pecan pie ($1/5$ of an 8 inch pie has 575 calories).

Chow down on a chocolate chip cookie (150 calories).

Nod off with a brandy (130 calories per $1^{1}/2$ ounces)

displayed, or don't go near the food until you are about to leave. Tell yourself you can have one piece of the delicious dessert or cheese, but you can have it only as you are leaving the party. That way, you will eat only one piece, not two or three. Stick to the healthier appetizers (usually hosts serve something that is relatively healthy, like veggies and dip) and keep talking! If you're in conversation, you won't eat as much and you won't feel as if you need to have something in your hands.

When you're on the go, stuff some healthy snacks into your purse, briefcase or the glove compart-

Take some healthy snacks with you

ment of your car so you don't rely on the snacks available from vending machines or convenience stores. Choose water, plain tea, coffee, or diet sodas over high-sugar drinks (which can be as many as 250 calories for one bottle). Look at the label before you eat or drink what's inside.

Tips for Eating Right at Restaurants

Most of us eat out occasionally, even often. At home, you are in control of how your food is prepared, but eating in a restaurant limits your control. You must focus, focus, focus (Chapter Seven) on what you need to eat and what you don't. When I eat out, I spend more time concentrating on ordering correctly, so I often eat better in restaurants than I do at home. I also ask that the chef prepare my meal the way I want it. I may not always get exactly what I ask for, but most restaurants attempt to please the customer. If you dine at a restaurant that seems to offer healthier choices or has a chef who is willing to accommodate your requests, choose that restaurant more often.

Here are a few more of my secrets for getting through a restaurant meal without sabotaging your whole day:

- Ask for meals like grilled fish or chicken with no fat or oil. Squeeze lemon over chicken or fish to add flavor without fat. Chefs always put some fat or oil in the dish, so ask for none and you will at least cut the amount back to a reasonable level.
- Order omelettes or egg dishes made with egg whites only. Most restaurants, even diners, do this regularly. The taste is the same and the calories, fat and cholesterol are greatly reduced.
- Order grilled vegetables on the side instead of pasta, rice or potatoes. Ask the waiter to have the vegetables prepared without fat, and cooked on the actual grill if possible—veggies are delicious prepared this way!
- Skip the rolls and especially crackers, which can pack a high-calorie punch for relatively little satisfaction. If your fellow diners don't mind, ask the waiter to remove the breadbasket.
- Order food without sauces or ask for them to be served on the side so you can measure how much to use. Always use a teaspoon to measure sauces or dressings. Add one teaspoon, and you may find that a small amount of sauce is enough. Also try dipping the tines of your fork into dressing or sauce and just eating a tiny bit with each bite.
- Instead of covering your salad with dressing, ask for balsamic vinegar. Most restaurants have it. Use a tea-

spoon full of dressing mixed with balsamic vinegar, or all vinegar if you like the taste of it. You can save 200 calories using this method.

- If you're eating out at a restaurant, consider leaving off certain ingredients, such as cheese or croutons, that don't add much taste to you but add a lot of calories. You will probably enjoy the dish just as much without that ingredient.
- Mix non-caloric condiments like Dijon mustard and vinegar with sugar substitute to make a no-calorie sauce or salad dressing.
- Don't order dessert. If someone else orders dessert and you can't resist it, have one or two bites and put your fork down. Concentrate on taking the last one or two bites from what is left after others have eaten it. A bite or two will probably satisfy your sweet tooth. Order a cup of coffee or tea with sugar substitute instead for a sweet meal finish.
- Don't try to starve yourself; eat your healthy food slowly and finish your meal if you want it. If you go home hungry, you will head straight to the cookie jar or the refrigerator and eat something totally unhealthy. Order healthy food and eat it!

If you develop and stick to an exercise program, you may think you need to eat a lot more food. But unless you're exercising like a professional athlete, you really don't need to eat much more. Add fresh fruit or carrots as a snack instead of a cookie or an ice cream bar when you feel hungry. When I look at what I can eat instead of one cookie (which can be anywhere from 50 to 150 calories) for the same calories (a whole bag of baby carrots or two pieces of fresh fruit), I'd rather have something with substance. Mainly, I eat fruit. Raw vegetables are great snacks, but they don't satisfy me.

Focus to Fight Temptation

Some days you can't resist eating high-calorie goodies. Any food eaten in moderation won't hurt you, so one doughnut every now and then is OK. Don't beat yourself up and eat everything else in sight because you have "ruined" your day. A doughnut is probably 200 calories, and an apple is 100 calories. So if you eat **Don't beat** the doughnut, don't eat the apple, too, and you're **yourself up** probably on track. You haven't messed up that badly. A treat is not something you have every day, but you deserve a treat once in a while. Life wouldn't be the same without them! But think seriously before you eat—think about what would really satisfy your current need and also keep your caloric intake under control.

When tempted, I use what I call the "apple test". Sometimes we eat just for the sake of eating, because it's there in front of our faces. I always say to myself, "Would an apple satisfy me? Am I so hungry that I would eat an apple right now?" Apples are sweet and crunchy, just like a lot of other snacks that aren't as healthy. So make sure you have an apple on hand when you need one. Buy apples or other tasty fruits at the market. Wash them when you get home so they'll be ready for easy snacking. Or put fresh apples or other fruits in a big bowl on your kitchen table. They look pretty and appetizing, and you won't forget to grab one when you need a snack. Or put each apple in an individual plastic bag in the refrigerator so you can grab one as you leave for work. Do what works for you. Give yourself a healthier option and make it easy to choose well.

I save calories just like I save money. A little bit here and there really adds up. Visualize your calories as a daily budget you must stay under in order to succeed. If you save a few pennies/calories, you'll be richer in the end. Share plates with a friend when you're out to lunch. Take some of your food home instead of eating the whole plate.

Save calories like you save money

It takes time to make changes in your eating habits. They won't happen overnight. Try to gradually adapt to a new way of eating and behaving. If you drink whole milk now, switch to two percent milk rather than skim. Eventually, you'll get used to the two percent milk and consider it normal. Then you should try to drink skim instead of two percent once in a while. Soon you'll enjoy skim milk just as much. It's a matter of habit.

Weight loss is something that happens gradually and naturally as you change to a healthy way of eating and consistent exercise. The impact on your attitude will be huge. You'll feel great about yourself when you can fit into smaller clothes sizes or when other people praise you. Keep going and you will be more confident, happier and more able to do the things you have always dreamed of doing. Set realistic, short-term goals for your weight loss so you don't feel discouraged. If you wish to lose thirty pounds in all, set a goal to lose two or three pounds a month. Don't try to lose ten pounds in one month—three pounds is more realistic. But those three pounds will make a huge difference in how you feel. If you lost three pounds every month, you would lose thirty-six pounds in a year!

The Road to Fitness: My Exercise Strategies

Like healthy eating, exercise is not a pursuit for only a month or two—it is a way of life and an essential element of a balanced life. Many people dislike exercising because they choose activities that are difficult or inconvenient, or they try to do too much at once. They soon burn out. A little bit of exercise is better than no exercise, so start off one day a week, and eventually it will get easier and you'll want to do more. Before you know it, exercise will become a habit, and you'll feel worse if you don't work-out according to your plan. If I don't exercise for two days, I feel really sluggish.

For my group of friends, fitness is very important. We feed off of each other's energy. I believe having a friend to diet and exercise with is key to eventual success. We know we have a date on the weekends to walk or run, and a designated time and place to meet. We don't chat on the phone; we save our stories for our run. So exercise becomes an obligation to my friends, not just a chore that I have to do.

Exercise has to be on my calendar, just like an important business meeting

I started running with some friends right when I was deciding to get a divorce from my first husband. These were two friends whom I wanted to confide in and get advice from about the life-changing decision I was about

Choose exercise you enjoy doing

to make. My regular running dates not only satisfied my exercise needs, but also gave me an opportunity to talk with my confidantes. I had been working out for about a year, but I had never run before. In April of that year, I could run three miles. By July 4th, I ran in the Peachtree Road Race, a 6.2-mile race in Atlanta. By that October, I was running in the Atlanta Half Marathon. It was a goal that I set, trained for and accomplished. I was so proud of myself! At an emotionally difficult time in my life, I did something positive for myself—something therapeutic for my mind and body.

Start exercising by choosing something that you enjoy doing and can easily work into your schedule. For some people, it might be walking in the neighborhood after work, or using the treadmill while watching TV. For others, it might mean joining a gym or an exercise class. Exercise classes such as step aerobics, jazz dancing or body sculpting are good for many people because they are fun, they're held on regular schedules, and they're usually free with a gym membership or at low cost through community centers and churches.

If you do join a gym, investigate the services of a personal trainer or exercise consultant. This is a true luxury, and not everyone can spare the expense. These professionals offer personalized advice and find ways to motivate you that work. If you can afford it, try using a trainer once a week for four weeks, and work out using the techniques he or she suggests when you're on your own. Then go to a trainer once a month or as often as you can. The trainer can guide your workouts so you achieve the maximum results. A trainer can be a good investment in yourself.

The Internet offers great exercise advice and even online personal trainers. These services are often far less expensive than face-to-face training. You simply enter your personal information (be honest!) and the online trainer creates a program for you and tracks your progress. Some gyms also offer free, computerized programs that track your progress.

A trainer can be a good investment in yourself

Again, make plans with friends to exercise or make friends in your exercise class so you are more inclined to show up. If you're absent, your friends will miss you and ask you where you were! If you pay for a trainer's services, you will be sure to show up. If you're self-conscious about your body or about exercising in front of others, consider buying a treadmill or other piece of personal exercise equipment. Use the reward system to keep yourself motivated. Give yourself a movie night with your best friend if you exercise four times on your treadmill, for example.

If you don't currently exercise, don't start off trying to exercise every day. You'll give up before you've made any positive impact and you might hurt yourself in the process. Start slowly, then build on your routines gradually. Exercise more often, for longer periods of time or at a higher level of exertion. Let's say you jog a regular route in 30 minutes. Time yourself and push harder so you run it in a shorter time—maybe 29 minutes. Each week, try to lower your time. Or add distance gradually—one more lap around the track or a few more blocks in your neighborhood.

Use rewards to motivate yourself

Add different types of exercise, such as strength training or various sports, to increase your fitness and keep your workouts interesting. I think a combination of cardiovascular activity (aero-

---

Reaching the Right Exercise Intensity

As you exercise, check your pulse about halfway into the most strenuous part of your workout and check your intensity level. Here's how:

1. Press two fingers lightly on the inside of your wrist or the lower part of your neck.
2. Look at a watch or clock with a second hand and count the number of beats you feel in 10 seconds.
3. Multiply by six to get your heart rate per minute.

For most of your workout, you want to stay within your target heart rate range for an effective cardiovascular workout. The American College of Sports Medicine has set the following guidelines for finding your target heart rate range:

- Take 220−your age = ___ (This is your maximum. The standard deviation for this equation is 10-12 beats per minute.)
- Determine your lower-limit exercise heart rate by multiplying your maximum heart rate by 0.6.
- Determine your upper-limit exercise rate heart by multiplying your maximum heart rate by 0.9.
- Your target heart rate range is between your upper and lower limits.

---

bics) and strength training (such as weightlifting) works best for achieving a fitter physique. Doing one thing all the time can be boring, and your body can also become used to it and not improve. To achieve **Start slowly,** fitness and build on it, you need to vary your routine **then build** and add new challenges. Soon you will make exercise a natural part of your everyday schedule.

A Few Great Strategies for Getting More (or Better) Exercise

- If you travel, don't sit around the hotel. Go outside for a run or walk and see the nearby sights. Explore or window shop on the streets as you exercise.
- Use the hotel's workout room (almost every hotel has one these days) and exercise while you watch the news or read the morning paper.
- If you're visiting family or in-laws during the holidays, use exercise as an excuse to escape the house for an hour or so. Go for a jog while your mother-in-law is cooking dinner.
- At home, go for walks or runs in new neighborhoods so you don't become bored with your routine. Look at new houses or shopping centers being built in your area.
- If you use a treadmill, vary your elevation each minute so you fight boredom and get a great workout.
- Listen to new music when you're working out at the gym, or try a book on tape. Many gyms now have workout machines with TV screens or CD players.

Everyday Activities/Calories Burned Per Hour

Activity	100 lb person	125 lb person	150 lb person	175 lb person	200 lb person
Mowing Lawn: push, power	216	270	324	378	432
Operate Snow Blower	216	270	324	378	432
Raking Lawn	192	240	288	330	384
Shoveling Snow by hand	288	360	432	504	576
Heavy Cleaning: Car,Windows	210	270	324	378	432
Moving: Carrying Boxes	338	420	504	588	672
Sitting: Reading or Watching TV	54	68	81	96	108
Sleeping (beats per minute.)	30	38	45	53	60

Individual & Non-team Sports/Calories Burned Per Hour

Activity	100 lb person	125 lb person	150 lb person	175 lb person	200 lb person
Bicycling: 14-16mph	480	600	720	840	960
Bowling	144	180	216	252	288
Golf: carrying clubs	264	330	396	462	520
Hiking: cross-country	238	360	432	504	576
Raquetball: compettitve	480	600	720	840	960
Running: 10 minutes	480	600	720	840	960
Tennis: general	336	420	504	580	672
Walking: 15 minutes	216	270	324	378	432

Water, Ice & Snow Sports/Calories Burned Per Hour

Activity	100 lb person	125 lb person	150 lb person	175 lb person	200 lb person
Skiing: downhill	288	360	432	504	576
Swimming: crawl	528	660	792	924	1056
Swimming: general	288	360	432	504	576

Team Sports/Calories Burned Per Hour

Activity	100 lb person	125 lb person	150 lb person	175 lb person	200 lb person
Basketball Game	384	480	576	672	760
Volleyball Game	384	480	576	672	760

Gym Activities/Calories Burned Per Hour

Activity	100 lb person	125 lb person	150 lb person	175 lb person	200 lb person
Aerobics, Step: high impact	480	600	720	840	960
Bicycling: stationary moderate	336	420	504	588	672
Circuit Training: general	384	480	576	672	760
StairStep Machine: general	288	360	432	505	570
Stretching: Hatha Yoga	192	240	288	336	384
Weight Lifting: general	144	180	216	252	288
Dancing: Disco, ballroom, square	204	330	386	402	528
Dancing: Fast, ballet, twist	288	380	432	504	576

Visit caloriecontrol.org/exercalc.html for a "Get Moving! Calculator" to see how many calories you expend doing your favorite exercise or activity. This calculator figures calories burned, based on your weight and exact number of minutes spent exercising.

- Use a heart rate monitor to test your exertion level when you are doing aerobic exercises like running, jogging, walking or working out on exercise machines. These devices are affordable and come with information on how to find your target heart rate range for optimum cardiovascular fitness. I recommend using these devices; it's also fun to see how hard your heart is working during exercise routines.
- If you used to enjoy sports like tennis, softball or golf when you were younger, pick them up again. Take some lessons and join a community league or start a regular game with friends. Sports can make exercise enjoyable and social to boot. You will be less likely to skip exercise if your friends or teammates depend on you, and you won't want to miss the fun.
- If you can read while you're doing aerobic exercise, you're not working hard enough. I prefer shorter harder workouts to longer slower workouts, but do what's best for you. If you're going to work out, why not exercise to your fullest potential? Get the most out of your workouts and see greater physical benefit.
- Exercise is something you must do for the rest of your life, so figure out what works for you and what you will stick with.
- Write a few details about your exercise in your calendar. If you stick with working out and build on what you do, you can look back and see how far you've come. This will motivate you to keep going.

Consistency is key in achieving fitness. I focus on my scheduled exercise a day in advance. If I do not have it planned in my head that at a certain time I will do a certain activity, I will find an excuse. I have to focus on my exercise and make it a priority. I recently started working out one day a week with a coach who emails me a weekly training schedule. This really works for me, because now I know what exercise I have to do every day. I've been training for duathalons, which include both running and biking, and right now I'm working on increasing my speed. When I started out, I was running a 10-minute mile. Now, in competition, I am running a less-than-8-minute mile.

Put exercise on your calendar

I could never have accomplished what I have if I had not focused. My weekly email reminders help to keep me focused, because I know what to do for how long and at what intensity. This level of exercise is not for everyone— I may have gone a little overboard—but I enjoy it and I've been winning competitions in my age group. It is the first time in my life that I find it truly pays to be older. I have achieved goals I never dreamed of reaching.

When you exercise, you have to visualize. Plan what exercise you will do today and include this activity as part of your daily schedule. Exercise has to be on my calendar, just like an important business meeting. Pack your gym bag before you leave the house and put it in your car so you'll have it when you leave work. Start with small goals, and then build on them. You'll see the results if you stick with it.

It's never too late to start exercising. I exercised infrequently until I was 37 years old. I played tennis but didn't do regular workouts or physical training. What made me start? I noticed changes in my body—my arms were starting to get soft underneath. Aging was my motivator. I felt that I could either work out and firm up or continue to look this way and maybe worse as time went on. I know people who believe that it's too late for them to get fit, or that fitness is a lost cause. They figure, why bother? But look around at the people you know or the people in your community. Look at the people over 70 who exercise regularly and compare them to those who don't. The regular exercisers look younger—maybe 15 years younger. The choice is yours.

- What unhealthy foods do you find most tempting? When do you find that you most lack willpower?

- What tricks can you use to avoid eating unhealthy foods in these situations?

- What keeps you from exercising regularly? How can you overcome these challenges? What changes can you make?

- How will you reward yourself for exercising regularly—something other than food?

Appendix

Epilogue

In this book, we've talked about ways to improve your attitude and achieve your goals. We've discussed how to think and act more positively, and how to live a healthier, more balanced life. You can go wherever you want to go if you only adopt the right mental approach to life—a positive, optimistic, hopeful one.

Of course you will have problems and setbacks. Of course you will encounter negative people who dismiss your efforts and try to discourage you. Of course you will have days when you don't feel like doing what you need to do to succeed. But the one thing that will help you overcome those obstacles—your very own pair of magic ruby slippers—is your attitude. Your attitude about yourself should be positive and confident. Your attitude about life should be hopeful and optimistic. Your attitude about your goals should be realistic but assertive. Go for what you really want, one little step at a time. If you have a healthy body to go with your healthy attitude, you are well equipped to succeed at anything you take on.

Life is just like the yellow brick road. It winds through many different settings. Some parts of the road take you through sunshine and flowers. Other parts ramble through dark forests full of lions, tigers and bears. Along the road, you will make many friends and encounter many challenges. But at the end of the journey is your ultimate destination—a happy life. Just like Dorothy, you hold the power to get there. That power is your attitude. It will take you wherever you want to go!

Acknowledgements

There are so many people that I would like to acknowledge for their roles in helping me create this book. Without them, there would be no *Attitude.*

At the top of that list is Susan Bernstein. She spent many hours listening to me, helping me to sort out my thoughts and get them on paper, and understanding what I wanted to say. We all have partners in life. Those that make us rise above what we are capable of is what a great partnership is – Thank you, Susan.

The other person who is important to this book that falls into the partner category is my husband, Richard, who lets me be myself and encourages me to always reach for the stars. I would also like to thank my daughters, Betsy and Jennifer. Words cannot describe how I feel about both of you. I think you know since I tell you all the time. You both make me very proud.

I also want to acknowledge some of the people who have had a tremendous impact on me over the last few years and those who have taken their time to help me with this book. Lauren, Garrett and Michelle, thanks for sharing your dad with me. Mom and Dad, you are my mentors and my greatest fans. Thank you for always being there for me in the good times and the bad.

To the rest of my family: You all mean so much to me. Nothing in my life is more important than my family and my friends. I want to thank my brother, Michael, who always gives me sound advice and only when I ask for it, and my sister, Karen, I know my secrets are always safe.

I want to thank Scott Bard, who is not only my publisher, but a true friend. I know if I really needed you, you would be there. It makes me feel safe.

And thank you to Chuck Perry, my editor, how you can change one word and clarify a whole section just amazes me.

To all of my friends: Thanks for all of your advice, thanks for always listening and encouraging me. And to those friends and my sister who read my book at various stages in the writing process – I am forever grateful – thanks for the feedback.

Also to everyone I ever worked with especially the staff at Chapter Eleven Bookstores without you I would not be where I am today.

Finally, thanks to the following for your guidance on making this book a reality: Lesley Gamwell, Spring Asher, Robyn Spizman, Tom Smolen, Gail Evans, Larry Kirshbaum, Gina Wright, Matt Russ, Alf Nucifora, Larry Liss, John Kelty, Karen Senft, and Susan Heidt.

Additional Reading

Here is a list of business books on various subjects, including leadership, motivation, management, financial savvy, and more-books that show us how we can tap into the power within, and to have a better attitude and a better life as a result.

Business:

Even a Geek Can Speak, Joey Asher
Who Moved My Cheese, Spencer Johnson
The Millionaire Next Door, Thomas Stanley
The Motley Fool Investment Guide, David Gardner
9 Steps to Financial Freedom, Suze Orman
The 7 Habits of Highly Effective People, Stephen Covey
22 Immutable Laws of Branding, Al Ries
What Color Is Your Parachute?, Richard Bolles
Tipping Point, Malcolm Gladwell
Good to Great, Jim Collins
Fish, Stephen Lundlin
Built From Scratch, Bernie Marcus
Jack: Straight from the Gut, Jack Welch
Raving Fans, Ken Blanchard
Purple Cow: Transform your Business by Being
The 10-Day MBA, Stephen Silbiger
The Present, Spencer Johnson
She Wins, You Win and *Play Like a Man, Win Like a Woman*, G. Evans

Networking:

Nonstop Networking, Andrea Nierenberg
Power Networking, Donna Fisher
Dig Your Well Before You're Thirsty, Harvey Mackay
How to Be a Star at Work, Robert Kelley
Masters of Networking, Ivan Misner

Balancing Your Life:

How Good People Make Tough Choices, R. M. Kidder
Balance Your Brain, Balance Your Life, Jay Lombard
Life Matters, A. Rodger Merrill
The Art of Happiness at Work, The Dalai Lama
There's No Such Thing As Business Ethics, John Maxwell
What Should I Do with My Life?, Po Bronson

Sales:

Be a Sales Superstar, Brian Tracy
How to Buy and Sell Just About Everything, Jeff Wuorio
Hug Your Customers, Jack Mitchell
Selling 101, Zig Ziglar
The 10 Immutable Laws of Selling, James Desena
The Sales Bible, Jeffrey Gitomer

Diet & Exercise:

The Zone, Barry Sears
Ultimate Fit or Fat, Covert Bailey
Atkins for Life, Robert Atkins, MD
Dr. Phil's Ultimate Weight Solution, Phil McGraw, PhD
Fit for Life, Not Fat for Life, Harvey Diamond
Suzanne Somers' Fast and Easy, Suzanne Somers
The South Beach Diet, Arthur Agatston, MD
The Tops Way to Weight Loss, Howard Rankin
Dr. Shapiro's Picture Perfect Weight Loss, Howard Shapiro, MD
Energy Addict, Jon Gordon

Fiction:

The Fountainhead and *Atlas Shrugged,* Ayn Rand
The Other Boleyn Girl, Philippa Gregory
Gloria, Keith Maillard
Greg Isles
Richard North Patterson
Ken Follett
Rick Bragg (His books are non-fiction, but read like fiction)
Younger Than That Now, Jeff Durstewitz
   (Also, non-fiction, but reads like fiction)
Terry Kay
William Diehl
Nelson DeMille (My favorite is *Charm School*)
The DaVinci Code, Dan Brown
The Haj, Leon Uris (Helps explain the Israeli-Palestinian Conflict, even
   though it was written about 20 years ago)
Kane and Abel, Jeffrey Archer
And: *A Girl's Guide to a Guy's World,* by my daughter, Jennifer Babbit –
   who was only 22 when she published this book
   (I guess a great attitude made it happen!)